Praise for *Lincoln and Emancipation*

"Part of the succinct yet illuminating [...] *and Emancipation* is a scholarly exa[...] Lincoln's perspective on slavery, from [...] the [...] Civil War (when he was open to a noninterference compromise if it would save the Union) to championing the cause of abolition before the conflict ended. *Lincoln and Emancipation* explores not only President Lincoln's words and ideology as they evolved over time, but also the voices of those who clamored for slavery's end: abolitionists and Radical Republicans, War Democrats, and both enslaved and free black people. Thought-provoking and expertly researched, *Lincoln and Emancipation* is a welcome addition to American History collections."   —*Midwest Book Review*

"Edna Greene Medford's new volume achieves a nearly impossible feat: a graceful and elegant synthesis of some of the best new scholarship on Lincoln's road to emancipation, a compact chronological outline of the political and policy shift highlights during the Civil War, and a narrative enriched with contemporary black voices and African American agency. Her solid and engaging study will prove invaluable to scholars and students alike, as this accessible and authoritative volume fills an important gap."

—**Catherine Clinton**, Denman Chair of American History, University of Texas at San Antonio

"Today's reassessment of 'the central act' of Lincoln's administration requires sound, thoughtful analysis, and Medford delivers. Prudently she separates myth from reality. Medford broadens emancipation history to embrace many active participants, including the impatient and fervent African Americans who agitated for freedom even before the United States of America was born. Just as emancipation ushered in an expectation of equality and fairness, today's general and diverse audience will appreciate that this work has something important to say about the construction of America's new birth of freedom."   —**Orville Vernon Burton**, author of *The Age of Lincoln*

CONCISE
LINCOLN
LIBRARY

—

EDITED BY RICHARD W. ETULAIN,
SARA VAUGHN GABBARD, AND
SYLVIA FRANK RODRIGUE

EDNA GREENE MEDFORD

Lincoln and Emancipation

Southern Illinois University Press
Carbondale

Southern Illinois University Press
www.siupress.com

23 22 21 20   4 3 2 1

The Concise Lincoln Library has been made possible
in part through a generous donation by the Leland E.
and LaRita R. Boren Trust.

Cover illustration adapted from a painting by Wendy
Allen

ISBN 978-0-8093-3796-5 (paperback)

The Library of Congress has cataloged the hardcover
edition as follows:
Medford, Edna Greene.
Lincoln and emancipation / Edna Greene Medford.
   pages cm
Includes bibliographical references and index.
ISBN 978-0-8093-3363-9 (cloth : alkaline paper)
ISBN 0-8093-3363-5 (cloth : alkaline paper)
ISBN 978-0-8093-3364-6 (ebook)
1. Lincoln, Abraham, 1809–1865—Political and social
views. 2. Lincoln, Abraham, 1809–1865—Relations
with African Americans. 3. Slaves—Emancipation—
United States. 4. Slavery—Political aspects—United
States—History—19th century. 5. African Americans—
Civil rights—History—19th century. 6. Equality—
United States—History—19th century. 7. United States—
Race relations—History—19th century. 8. United
States—Politics and government—1861–1865. I. Title.
E457.2M497 2015
973.7092—dc23   2014033618

For Tom

CONTENTS

Gallery of illustrations following page 60

LINCOLN AND EMANCIPATION

INTRODUCTION

The year 1800 and the decade following foreshadowed the struggle over slavery that would eventually engulf the nation by midcentury. On August 30, Gabriel, the human property of Thomas Prosser of Henrico County, Virginia, attempted to strike out against nearly two centuries of racial injustice and inhumanity by gathering in rebellion a thousand or more enslaved people from the countryside surrounding Richmond. Of imposing stature at nearly six feet, three inches tall, the literate blacksmith had come to the attention of the courts because of his fight with a white overseer a year earlier. Gabriel had been convicted of maiming (he had bitten off most of the overseer's ear), a capital offense. His sentence was commuted to burning in the hand, but the punishment meted out for this violation of Virginia laws had not subdued him.

Gabriel's revolt had been meticulously planned. The men would arm themselves with swords made from scythes and with weapons seized from the arsenal. They would take hostages (including Governor James Monroe, the future president of a nation that was then just over two decades old) and attack Richmond. But in the end, this would-be army of liberation was stayed by the unpredictability of nature—torrential rains hindered access to the city arsenal—and by the treachery of two of Gabriel's compatriots. After escaping to Norfolk, the audacious slave was captured, tried, convicted, and executed, the fate reserved for all who dared to employ violence in defense of black freedom. More than two dozen of his fellow conspirators shared his destiny. One of them, likening his actions to that of the American colonists in the Revolution, declared that he had "nothing more to offer than what general Washington would have had to offer had he been taken by the British and put to trial by them. I have adventured my life in endeavoring to obtain the liberty of my country men and am a willing sacrifice in their cause."[1]

Bracketing Gabriel's attempted revolt was the birth of two men, one a white man who believed God had called him to liberate those held in bondage and the other an enslaved man. Born in May, John Brown would spend much of his adult life fighting for the freedom of a people with whom his only connection was a shared humanity. The brutality of his tactics against supporters of slavery and his uncompromising commitment to freedom led men and women in his own time to question his sanity. His mental stability remains a source of interest and debate even today.

Later in the year, Nat, the property of Benjamin Turner of Southampton County, Virginia, drew his first breath. Encouraged in the belief by those around him (black and white) that he was special, the boy grew into manhood certain, like John Brown, that God had created him for some great purpose. By the time he was thirty-one, the literate preacher had garnered as much respect from his presumed superiors as was possible for an enslaved person. But Nat had no interest in seeking the favor of white men. After receiving what he believed to be God's plan for him through a series of visions, he would take his turn as liberator of his people. On August 22 and 23, 1831, he led a small band in rebellion through Southside Virginia before the alarmed community rallied to quash his attack.[2] Captured after two months in hiding, he met his death at the hands of state officials who considered him property but nevertheless held him accountable for his actions.[3] Dozens more, many of them totally innocent of any crime, met their end at the hands of white vigilantes overcome with fear and the realization that all was not well with their enslaved laborers.

In a sense, Denmark Vesey was "born" in 1800 as well. That year the former slave had purchased his freedom using funds he had won earlier in the South Carolina lottery. His industriousness and skill at carpentry afforded him a comfortable life, but he suffered the inhumanity of separation from family members who remained in slavery. Twenty-two years after he had secured his own freedom, he would plan a revolt that would have been the largest in the history of the nation, had the plot not been uncovered beforehand.

Born within a decade of this watershed year, Abraham Lincoln represented a different kind of defender of freedom, one who eschewed violence but, ironically, would help to destroy slavery by militarily defending the American Union. Lincoln followed a less urgent and more detached path than the revolutionaries. While he saw advantage in gradual and peaceful abolition, the war escalated his timetable and altered his approach.

Understanding the man who would be credited with freeing the slaves requires the separation of myth from reality, a task not so easily achieved when dealing with Lincoln. A century and a half after his death, he remains an enigma, not fully understood even by those who think they know him best. Thousands of books have addressed every conceivable aspect of his life, yet his motivations and actions in the effort to end slavery remain contested ground.[4] The sesquicentennial observance of the issuing of his Emancipation Proclamation has only heightened our interest and has encouraged reassessments of the "central act" of his administration. Hence, the last decade has witnessed the publication of several volumes that view him from intriguing, and often provocative, perspectives. Books depict Lincoln committed to ending slavery from early on in the war and being able to succeed by prudently negotiating the challenges he faced from Peace Democrats, both conservative and radical members of his own party, border state representatives, and constraints placed on him by the Constitution.[5] Other works discuss his evolving views about international laws of war and how they might have provided a legal framework for emancipation.[6] And in a movement away from the traditional focus on Lincoln as the sole architect of emancipation, his actions are presented as a continuation of a larger Republican strategy, which had originated and developed from the party's antislavery policies that predated the war. Viewed through this lens, southern suspicions of a Republican president were justified.[7]

These works, and others, have contributed immeasurably to the discourse surrounding slavery, emancipation, and Lincoln's role in America's struggle with its own principles in the mid-nineteenth century.[8] While this volume takes a traditional approach to interpreting the destruction of slavery—it is grounded in the notion that union was indeed paramount in the president's thinking and that slavery's demise (whether by military or by state action) resulted as a consequence of war—its primary aim is to broaden the emancipation narrative. While Lincoln remains central to the story, it argues for the inclusion of many players in the drama—among them, the abolitionists and Radical Republicans, War Democrats, and others (including the Gabriels, Veseys, Nats, and John Browns) who pushed America to complete the transition begun by those who had championed liberty in 1776.

To this end, the volume seeks to restore African Americans to their rightful place in the struggle for their own liberation. The historiography is rather uneven in regard to how emancipation studies choose to depict the beneficiaries of freedom, with extremes that either suggest they made minor contributions to their liberation or argue for the primacy of self-emancipation. An alternative way of viewing emancipation, perhaps, is that the president and the seekers of freedom constituted an informal, if sometimes strained, alliance based on the self-interest of both. Lincoln was not a protector of slavery, but neither were enslaved men and women peripheral to the process; they were much more than a "species of property" waiting patiently to be transformed into human beings by presidential decree. By acting in their own self-interest, African Americans facilitated Lincoln's emancipation plans and sometimes extended them. They were fervent, impatient participants in the emancipation effort, showing an eagerness to get on with the business of freedom long before the rest of the country had embraced their cause. But in the end, their goal merged with Lincoln's, and together they achieved in deed the liberty that Americans had heretofore championed in word.

CHAPTER ONE

THE MAN AND HIS TIMES

On the eve of the Civil War the existence of slavery was accepted by great numbers of Americans as a normal (and by some, even a necessary) feature of American society. Even among those northerners most troubled by the South's peculiar institution, few were prepared to welcome black men and women into their cities and towns as fellow Americans, free to come and go as they pleased, to live where they wished, and to seek gainful employment. Yet, some twenty months into the war, Abraham Lincoln had taken the extraordinary step of declaring enslaved people free. Not quite three years later, Americans would ratify a constitutional amendment that forever outlawed one person's ownership of another. This reversal in American attitudes reflected the influence of a searing focus on the expansion of slavery that was decades long and had culminated in the crisis of disunion and civil war. Few were more affected by the crisis than the national executive, and for the next four years, starting with the shots at Fort Sumter, it compelled him to challenge old assumptions and to embrace new ideas based on national interest.

Those old assumptions had themselves been shaped by circumstance, resulting from tensions between espoused American ideals and certain realities in American society in the first half of the nineteenth century. The still young nation had attracted worldwide attention and had drawn the inquisitive to its shores. Among them was the young French aristocrat Alexis de Tocqueville, who visited the United States during 1831 and 1832, when Lincoln was coming of age. Tocqueville was intrigued by the implications of American democracy and its potential impact on political and social developments in the rest of the world. Having secured permission and funding from his government to tour the United States for the purpose of observing its penal system, which was being transformed in the midst of the great reform movements of the antebellum era, he and companion Gustave de Beaumont traveled across America over a nine-month period. They elbowed their way through the bustling, crowded, and often squalid northern cities; took in the placid landscape of the countryside; encountered the human property of the plantation South; trudged through the wilderness that was the western frontier; and journeyed to the sparsely populated but rapidly evolving towns of the heartland.

Tocqueville made detailed observations of the new democracy, sometimes offering a less than flattering image of his host nation. He found that Americans, generally, were a very ambitious and restless lot who were always looking for the next, better opportunity. In Tocqueville's estimation, an American "clutches everything, he holds nothing fast, but soon loosens his grasp to pursue fresh gratifications." In America "a man builds a house in which to spend his old age, and he sells it before the roof is on; he plants a garden and lets it just as the trees are coming into bearing; he brings a field into tillage and leaves other men to gather the crops."[1]

Tocqueville found in the America of Lincoln's youth the disturbing existence of a "tyranny" or "despotism of the majority" that threatened individual liberty. "I know no country in which there is so little true independence of mind and freedom of discussion as in America," he wrote. This "tyranny of the majority" affected not only public opinion but political thought as well. The Frenchman claimed to be less concerned with the "excessive liberty" that characterized America as with "the very inadequate securities which exist against tyranny."[2]

Perhaps what intrigued Tocqueville most was the supposed fluidity of American society, the idea that a condition of equality existed among the people. He observed that servants (white ones, that is) considered themselves equal to their employers and could aspire to the status of those for whom they labored.³ But social fluidity had its limits, even in America. The nation, after all, was composed of a heterogeneous population, a place where perceived inferior races lived alongside a perceived superior one. Tocqueville noted that people of color were barred from taking part fully and equally in American society by the "almost insurmountable barriers" of education, the law, customs, and physical characteristics. They suffered from the very real "tyranny" of white men.⁴

In his travels through America, Tocqueville encountered remnants of the great Native tribes of the North as well as those in the states that would become the future Confederacy. The experience left him saddened that "savage" but noble beings had been so thoroughly ravaged by their interactions with the Europeans. At Memphis he witnessed the forced emigration of the Choctaws—in the middle of winter, their sick and infirm, women and children trudging behind them—as they crossed the Mississippi, making their way to uncertainty in the West. "[T]he tyranny of the States obliges the savages to retire, the Union, by its promises and resources, facilitates their retreat; and these measures tend to precisely the same end,"⁵ which Tocqueville concluded was the eventual extermination of the Indian.

Tocqueville's response to the condition of African Americans was less sympathetic. He claimed (incorrectly) that the enslaved African had rejected the religion and customs of his ancestors when he was brought to America and had regressed into a pathetic being who "admires his tyrants more than he hates them, and finds his joy and his pride in the servile imitation of those who oppress him; his understanding is degraded to the level of his soul." However misinformed he was about African American culture and behavior, he was prophetic in his assessment of the potential danger that slavery posed to the nation: "The most formidable of all the ills which threaten the future existence of the Union arises from the presence of a black population upon its territory." Moreover, abolition did not improve race relations. Where slavery had been removed, the races did not coexist on terms equally favorable to both. He found that white Americans had a deep-seated prejudice against people of color and that the prejudice increased the farther removed one got from slavery. Hence, racial biases appeared to be "stronger in the States which have abolished slavery, than in those where it still exists; and nowhere is it so intolerant as in those States where servitude has never been known."[6]

Tocqueville's visit to America coincided with increasing tensions over slavery. The northern states had divested from the institution in the wake of the American Revolution, while southerners had strengthened its grip on their society. By the time Lincoln entered adulthood, slavery had been eradicated from Maine to Pennsylvania, but its survival in the South divided the nation between two competing visions of America's future.

As Tocqueville observed, the abolition of slavery did not result in equality in the northern states. "The negro is free," he wrote, "but he can share neither the rights nor the pleasures, nor the labor, nor the afflictions, nor the tomb of him whose equal he has been declared to be; and he cannot meet him upon fair terms in life or in death." While free black men had enjoyed voting rights in several of the states in the years following the Revolution, by the 1830s, all except the New England states had enacted legislation that prevented black men from participating in the political process or severely restricted their access. Free black men and women were denied equal treatment in the courts as well. In many states, laws prevented them from testifying in cases involving a white person, from serving on juries, or from being heard by a jury of their peers.[7]

Nor did free African Americans enjoy social equality or economic opportunity in Lincoln's America. They faced segregation and discrimination in public accommodations and unequal access to educational institutions. Free black men and women suffered restricted theater seating, segregation in hospitals and in churches, and separation in death from white residents of towns and cities. As members of a despised race, they were expected to find employment in the lowest paying and least desirable jobs, and they frequently were forced to surrender even those to immigrants seeking asylum from the crushing poverty of their own homelands. Lamenting the disabilities under which free black people were forced to live, Clarissa Lawrence, president of the Colored Female Religious and Moral

Society of Salem, Massachusetts, charged, "We meet the monster prejudice every where. We cannot elevate ourselves. . . . Prejudice is the cause. . . . [It] follows us every where, even to the grave. . . . We are blamed for not filling useful places in society, but . . . give us learning, and see then what places we will occupy."[8]

The majority of African Americans, of course, lived under the devastating weight of bondage. They labored in the cultivation of tobacco and cereal grains in Maryland and Virginia; tended the rice and cotton fields in South Carolina, Georgia, and Mississippi; cut cane and sweltered in the boiling houses of sugar-producing Louisiana; and worked in all sorts of nonagricultural labor. Soil exhaustion in the Upper South encouraged the transfer of enslaved people to the Lower South, where the expansion of cotton production absorbed large numbers of laborers. This domestic slave trade increased the suffering of black people as husbands were separated from wives and parents from children. In the South the free black population grew slowly as the enslaved population surged. Whether in the city or countryside, the majority of free black people lived and labored wherever they could, sometimes alongside enslaved men and women, where they occupied dwellings of no better quality.

By 1830 the condition of free African Americans was so deplorable that leaders (a small black elite that had escaped the poverty of the vast majority) organized annual meetings to address the most serious concerns. These conventions called primarily for cooperation among free people of color to pressure national and state governments to grant them the rights they felt they were due by birth. Specifically, they agitated for the elective franchise, equal access to public accommodations, and schools that would help to transform the masses from menial laborers. Although very much focused on their own elevation, northern free people of color recognized the connection between their own well-being and the elimination of slavery. Hence, humanitarianism and self-interest combined to encourage them to press for abolition as well.[9]

The black convention movement represented a more general activism that swept the country during the 1820s, 1830s, and 1840s. Encouraged by the egalitarian rhetoric of democracy, a growing political voice for the common man and economic upheaval, reformist groups of Americans worked to eradicate the system that denied liberty to African Americans and limited the opportunities of white men from the lower classes. Abolitionism became increasingly regional, as the effort undertaken by men and women in the North came to be viewed as an affront to southerners and an assault on their cherished social and economic institutions. Political parties took positions on the matter; a few, such as the Liberty and the Free Soil Parties, were formed for the purpose of agitating for emancipation of the enslaved or to prevent the expansion of slavery into the territories. Other men and women, such as the followers of William Lloyd Garrison, who considered the Constitution to be a proslavery document, elected to agitate for freedom outside of the political arena.[10] But despite these challenges to the status quo, freedom remained elusive. Slaveholders in the national government and their friends north and south stifled any attempt at universal abolition. And rather than being seen as champions of American values, abolitionists faced condemnation as troublemakers and were subjected to verbal abuse and physical attack.

Not all of the effort to liberate the bondman and bondwoman came from outside forces. Enslaved people themselves challenged the system in myriad ways. Nat Turner's Rebellion, which took place during Tocqueville's visit, is but one example. The incident forced Virginians to rethink practices of more than a century and a half. For a brief moment, the legislature considered eliminating slavery through gradual means, but in the end it chose to strengthen the laws regulating both the enslaved population and free people of color. The new legislation restricted the movement of African Americans, as well as prohibited education and assembly. It limited the number of people who could gather socially and made a white man's presence at black church services mandatory. It became illegal to teach an enslaved person *or* a free black person to read.[11]

Lincoln's ideas about race, freedom, and equality were formed in this increasingly sectional America. It remains unclear how much of his aversion to slavery emanated from childhood experiences. Although he recalled in 1860 that his father had moved the family to Indiana "partly on account of slavery," recent scholarship would suggest that the elder Lincoln's motivations were a bit more complex.[12] Lincoln spent his childhood in places where slavery, at the very least, was a topic for discussion if not an economic nuisance to the nonplanter population. While hardly a "black belt" when the Lincoln family lived there, Hardin County, Kentucky, had more than a thousand enslaved people in 1816 when the Lincolns departed for Indiana.[13] Thomas Lincoln may very well have felt economically challenged by the presence of enslaved laborers. As a carpenter and farmer, he would have found it hard to supplement his meager earnings from farming his own land with the wages that he might earn by hiring himself out to neighbors. Lincoln claimed that the relocation occurred "chiefly on account of the difficulty in land titles in Ky." Thomas had experienced trouble acquiring clear title to three parcels of land in the state, which would have made Indiana with its more rigorous process for titling land more attractive.[14]

Nor is it clear how much interaction with African Americans Lincoln would have experienced in Indiana. A part of the Northwest Territory where slavery was prohibited by the Ordinance of 1787, Indiana officially outlawed the institution by constitutional means when the state gained admission to the Union the very same year that the Lincolns arrived. Yet human bondage continued to taint the society for several more years. The early settlers who had occupied the land before it was ceded to the British as a consequence of French defeat in the French and Indian War were allowed to retain their property. Unfree labor was strengthened by a law passed by the territorial legislature in 1807, which legalized indentured servitude; settlers, in turn, found ways to extend terms of indenture to lifetime service. Despite the existence of antislavery laws, officials ignored the flagrant disregard and misinterpretation of such legislation. Moreover, certain Indiana residents, among them the territorial governor at the time, Virginia-born William Henry Harrison, launched a sustained proslavery campaign. Harrison used every resource at his disposal to implement slavery legally, but antislavery forces succeeded in keeping the proslavery groups in check. Still, pockets of slavery existed well into the antebellum period.[15]

Although he may not have encountered slavery in Indiana, Lincoln did experience its ugliness while residing in the state. In 1828, at the age of nineteen, he was hired to ferry a cargo of goods down the Mississippi River to New Orleans. Along the way, he and his partner traded at several sugar plantations, where Lincoln would have had the opportunity to observe the institution. The trip placed him in danger, as one night the two tied up their flatboat at a riverside plantation a few miles south of Baton Rouge. During the night, several presumably enslaved black men who aimed to rob them attacked the pair. After a brief struggle Lincoln and his fellow crewman repelled the men, and the flatboat continued its journey down the Mississippi. History does not record what Lincoln and his companion encountered once in New Orleans, but tradition has it that they witnessed a slave auction while in the city, an incident that disturbed Lincoln greatly. His future law partner William Herndon would later recount a story about what the young Lincoln quipped: "If ever I get a chance to hit that thing [meaning slavery], I will hit it hard."[16]

A short time thereafter, Lincoln moved with his family to Illinois, where as in Indiana slavery existed as the result of a loophole. Proslavery forces had pressed to keep the institution in the state, despite laws to the contrary. While it held territorial status, Illinois had permitted the importation of enslaved laborers for the saltworks at Shawneetown (located in southeastern Illinois, on the Ohio River). The constitution of 1818, adopted when the state was admitted to the Union, outlawed any further introduction of slavery and involuntary servitude, except as punishment for crime. Yet, for the next several decades, the state clearly exhibited a proslavery, antiblack bias. First, it stipulated that those persons already held to labor were required to abide by the terms of their contracts or indentures; their children would be freed when they reached the age of majority (twenty-one for men and eighteen for women). Subsequent laws prevented enslaved people from seeking asylum in Illinois and discouraged abolitionist activity by imposing fines on anyone who brought an enslaved laborer into the state for the purpose of freeing him or her from bondage.[17] The Illinois codes restricted the internal movement of African Americans by requiring passes and severely limiting the number of people who could assemble in any one place. The laws also sought to punish those white men and women who "conspired" with an enslaved person to disobey the law.

Free black Illinoisans were vulnerable to the state's laws as well. As with the southern states, the "black codes" required African Americans to show evidence of freedom by presenting certificates of such to the county clerk, who then registered the person and recorded his physical description. Failure to produce freedom papers subjected the person to arrest. Free black people were also required by law to post a bond in the amount of one thousand dollars—an impossible requirement for most working-class people (white or black)—ostensibly as insurance against becoming indigent and hence a burden to the community. In 1853 the state attempted to prohibit black immigration altogether by imposing a fine on those who arrived with the intention to reside there permanently. If such a person was unable to pay the fifty-dollar fine, the sheriff was authorized to auction off his or her labor to whoever was willing to pay it.[18]

The debate over slavery had taken center stage long before Lincoln arrived. In 1822, when proslavery advocates proposed a constitutional convention that would draft a proslavery document, Illinois' governor, Edward Coles, himself a former slave owner who had freed his property, led the opposition in defeat of the attempt.[19] Other men spoke out against slavery in the press and from the pulpit. One of them, Elijah Lovejoy, resident of Alton and editor of the *Alton Observer*, paid with his life in 1837 while defending his printing press from an anti-abolitionist mob. Before his death, Lovejoy had helped to establish the Illinois Anti-Slavery Society.

Lincoln joined the debate over slavery in the 1830s, after having secured a seat in the Illinois legislature. In 1837 the General Assembly had responded to increasing national concerns over the pressure that was being exerted by abolitionists regarding the issue of slavery. As several other states voiced their objections to such pressures, Illinois offered its own position on the matter. In March the legislature passed a resolution criticizing abolition societies and condemning their principles. The same resolution confirmed the constitutional right of slaveholders to their human property and denied that they could be separated from that property against their will. Taking up the issue of Congress's control over the District of Columbia, the Illinois legislature avowed that slavery could not be abolished in the federal city without the consent of the people residing there.[20]

Only six of the legislators, including Lincoln, objected to the conservative pronouncements. Voting contrarily with Lincoln was fellow Sangamon County representative Dan Stone. The men's objections, far from being a radical departure from the majority, stated simply that "the institution of slavery is founded on both injustice and bad policy" but "the Congress of the United States has no power, under the constitution, to interfere with the institution of slavery in the different States." And although Congress *did* have the authority to abolish slavery in the District of Columbia, such power should be utilized only with the consent of the people who lived there. Finally, the "antislavery" men asserted that abolitionist doctrines exacerbated the evils of slavery rather than reduced them.[21] As Tocqueville had observed, few were willing to venture out too far in front of the majority.

Lincoln's views on slavery reflected prevailing Whig ideology. Formed in opposition to the power and political sentiment of Andrew Jackson and the Jacksonians, the Whigs drew their party membership from a diverse America—southern planters, yeoman farmers on the frontier, northern businessmen, and reform-minded urban dwellers. They supported a strong central government, internal improvements that would enable westerners to get their goods to eastern markets, a sound national banking system, and protective tariffs for fledgling American industries. The reform-minded wing of the party often expressed its antislavery sentiment, not simply because the institution was considered immoral but because it stood in the way of progress for white men and ran contrary to America's democratic and egalitarian principles.

Lincoln's "beau ideal of a statesman" was the Whig leader Henry Clay, who represented Kentucky in both houses of Congress for many years and was Speaker of the House for three terms. Clay embodied the contradictory, but not unusual, practice in nineteenth-century America of being antislavery while owning human property. Such men (and women) attempted to reconcile this hypocrisy by employing convoluted logic. Clay best epitomized this practice. Invited to an antislavery rally in Indiana in 1842, he sought to ensure the audience that he identified with their view of slavery as "a great evil." But since it was a legally sanctioned institution, he argued, nothing could be done to get rid of it. Appealing to the prejudices and fears of many Americans in the North and West, he argued that "far greater evils . . . would inevitably flow from a sudden, general, and indiscriminate emancipation." Those evils involved amalgamation, "that revolting admixture alike offensive to God and man." The mixing of the races would lead to civil war, carnage, pillage, devastation, and the ultimate extermination or expulsion of black people. Even the enslaved benefited from a more gradual approach to emancipation, he reasoned. Some enslaved people, because of age or infirmity, could not take care of themselves, and hence it would be unchristian to turn them out. Besides, Clay argued, there were those who did not even want to be freed. Slavery was mild and the conditions of the bondman had continually improved. If some owners had thought it necessary to become more rigid, it was because the abolitionists were stirring up the enslaved population and promoting insurrection.[22]

Clay counseled the use of this argument in 1843 as a strategy to counter the abolitionists. "It is manifest that the ultras of that party are extremely mischievous, and are hurrying on the country to fearful consequences," he wrote to his official biographer, the minister-turned-author Calvin Colton. To arrest their progress, he suggested that a tract be written, the main tactic of which was to turn the laboring classes in the North against abolitionism by highlighting the consequences of immediate emancipation: "The slaves, being free, would be dispersed throughout the Union. They would enter into competition with the free laborer; with the American, the Irish, the German; reduce his wages; be confounded with him, and affect his moral and social standing." Clay advised that proslavery supporters should also use the amalgamation argument to "show that their [the abolitionists] object is to unite, in marriage, the laboring white man and the laboring black man, and to reduce the white laboring man to the despised and degraded condition of the black man." This theme of amalgamation continued in Clay's advice to question the abolitionists' opposition to colonization, a solution to the race problem that he championed as a founding member of the American Colonization Society. "Why do the Abolitionists oppose colonization?" he asked. "To keep and amalgamate together the two races in violation of God's will and to keep the blacks here, that they may interfere with, degrade, and debase the laboring whites. . . . You can make a powerful article that will be felt in every extremity of the Union."[23]

Clay's imprint on Lincoln's thinking would be reflected in the way the latter viewed and responded to the slavery question in the decades preceding the Civil War. As a one-term member of the House of Representatives, the future president became involved in the debate over slavery in the nation's capital. The institution and the domestic trade that was its by-product had been a source of embarrassment to many of those who visited or lived in the city or participated in national lawmaking. Years after he had left Congress, Lincoln would recall that one could witness "in full view from the windows of the capitol, a sort of negro livery stable where droves of negroes were collected, temporarily kept, and finally taken to southern markets, precisely like droves of horses."[24] Attempts had been made to abolish the institution or ban the trade, but the slave power and its support-ers managed to derail any and all efforts. In 1848 the *Pearl* incident graphically illuminated the plight of the enslaved in the District of Columbia. On the night of April 15, seventy-seven men, women, and children made their way to the city dock and boarded a schooner bound for the North. Their escape thwarted by becalmed winds, they were returned to the city amid loud protests against abolitionists and other inciters of rebellion.[25] Many of the captured fugitives were sold and transported to the Deep South, including two teenage girls, Em-ily and Mary Edmonson, whose plight soon drew national attention.

The sight of well-mannered, dignified enslaved domestics being shipped off to some hellish unknown convinced antislavery locals and congressmen that the time had come to put an end to the trade in human commodities in the nation's capital. The debate that followed was contentious, with little hope for successfully bridging the divide. Lincoln offered a compromise resolution that, had it been adopted, would have eliminated slavery from the city. Abolition would have been achieved gradually and with the consent of the owners. The resolution held that slaveholders would be compensated for the loss of their property. Children born to women still enslaved on January 1, 1850, would be required to work for the mother's owner until they reached an as yet unspecified age and would be educated and supported according to apprenticeship laws. The resolution sought to prevent the District from becoming a haven for fugitives from nearby Maryland and Virginia plantations by stipulating the arrest of anyone attempting to flee to the city. But Lincoln discarded the resolution when he failed to receive the support that had been promised.[26]

When his congressional term ended, Lincoln returned to Springfield and resumed his law practice with William Herndon as his partner. During this period the two participated as counsel in cases where free and enslaved African Americans were either plaintiffs or defendants, but such instances were not numerous. In his entire legal career, only thirty-four of the five thousand cases in which he participated involved African Americans, and they did not reveal any special concern for promoting universal black freedom.[27] In the case *People v. Hill*, for instance, the defendant, Isabella Hill, a free black woman who had been summoned "on a recognizance for keeping the peace," retained him and Herndon.[28] The firm also represented the black woman Mary Shelby in the case *Shelby v. Freeman and Freeman*, which involved a land dispute. A decade earlier, Lincoln had represented Mary Shelby in her suit against her husband, Mack, from whom she sought a divorce. In at least two instances, Lincoln and Herndon represented Springfield's black barber, William Fleurville (or Florville), with whom the two men (especially Lincoln) had been acquainted. In *Florville v. Allin et al.*, the black man sued three white men for conveyance of a deed. Lincoln paid most of the court costs himself. *Florville v. Stockdale et al.* also involved a land dispute. Fleurville won the suit, but it is not clear that he ever received title to the disputed land.[29]

Unquestionably, the most controversial and confounding of Lincoln's cases involving African Americans is *In re Bryant et al.* The plaintiff, slaveholder Robert Matson of Kentucky, was charged with transporting five of his enslaved laborers to Illinois, where, in violation of the statute regarding slaves in transit, he domiciled them for two years. With the help of sympathetic local residents, Jane Bryant sued for freedom on behalf of herself and her four children, but Matson declared them to be runaways and retained Lincoln to help him retrieve his property. The family was arrested and brought to trial, where the future architect of the Emancipation Proclamation represented his client's interests by arguing that the enslaved family was in transit and hence Matson had not violated the law. The court rejected Lincoln's argument and freed the family.[30]

The Matson case, perhaps more than any other, conveys the complexity of Lincoln's attitudes about slavery and its place in American society. His thinking was shaped by two opposing ideas: first, that enslaved people were human beings entitled to basic rights, and second, that they were property, protected as such by the Constitution. Lincoln believed that the framers of that document and the members of the earliest Congress tolerated slavery "only by necessity" and intended that ultimately it would become extinct. In an effort to hide the existence of slavery, to keep the idea of "property in man" out of the Constitution, the framers excluded the words "slave" and "slavery" and instead employed euphemisms such as "persons" from whom "service or labor . . . may be due."[31]

Lincoln had always acknowledged Congress's lack of authority to control or abolish slavery in the various states, but he believed that the Constitution authorized the national legislature to prevent the institution from spreading into the territories. So, as the debate over slavery intensified in the decade preceding the Civil War, he pressed for its containment in the areas where it already existed. This anti-expansion position made him a moderate in an increasingly volatile discourse. While still in Congress he had witnessed the debate over the disposition of lands acquired by the United States in the 1846–48 war with Mexico. When Pennsylvania congressman David Wilmot proposed a measure blocking the extension of slavery into any of the territory acquired from Mexico, Lincoln supported it, but he did not engage in the heated debates that the proviso touched off in Congress during his term there.[32]

The divide between antislavery and proslavery forces reached critical mass in 1854 over the issue of the organization of territorial governments in Kansas and Nebraska. Congress's decision to repeal the Missouri Compromise and allow Kansas residents to decide the issue of whether they wanted the state to be slave or free destroyed the Whig Party and severely hobbled the Democrats. When a new political entity—the Republican Party—was formed, Lincoln embraced its commitment to excluding slavery from the territories and containing it where it already existed.

The Kansas-Nebraska crisis afforded Lincoln the opportunity to develop and share his views on slavery and its future in American society. In his address at Peoria in October 1854, he outlined his objections to the Kansas-Nebraska Act and to the extension of slavery westward into the territories. Lincoln believed slavery to be a "monstrous injustice" that "enables the enemies of free institutions, with plausibility, to taunt us as hypocrites—causes the real friends of freedom to doubt our sincerity." In the early days of the republic, Congress sought to control the trade in enslaved people in a way that would retard its growth, rather than attempted to achieve the impossible task of eradicating it outright.[33] To allow its extension into the territories would encourage its existence everywhere, increase the demand for enslaved laborers, and ultimately lead to the reopening of the transatlantic trade in human beings. Lincoln argued further that the western territory should be reserved for free white men and women. This could not happen if slavery was allowed to enter the area. "Slave States are places for poor white people to remove FROM," he argued, "not to remove TO. New free States are the places for poor people to go to and better their condition."[34]

Since owners of enslaved people had a constitutional right to their property, they were entitled to legislation that permitted them to reclaim runaways. Lincoln thought the Fugitive Slave Act "a sort of dirty, disagreeable job" that was degrading to the free states, in that it obliged them to engage in the apprehension of fugitives. Yet he did not object to it as long as its enforcement was no more "likely to carry a free man into slavery, than our ordinary criminal laws are to hang an innocent one."[35]

Lincoln's support for the Fugitive Slave Act was a position that would separate him from African Americans in the 1850s and into the first year of the Civil War. African American opposition to the proslavery measure followed swiftly on the heels of its having passed in Congress. The law was no mere inconvenience to people whose freedom had no legal standing. Before 1850, fugitives could relocate in the North with some degree of assurance that they would be far removed from the slave catcher's grasp. The law passed in 1850 left them apprehensive. It required private citizens as well as law enforcement officers to cooperate in the apprehension of runaways. Failure to do so or aiding or hiding suspected fugitives or allowing them to escape could result in a fine and/or imprisonment.[36] Despite the enactment of personal liberty laws to counter the act, runaways who had lived without fear in the North for years now felt compelled to leave the country entirely. The exodus to Canada in the decade before the Civil War attests to the seriousness with which African Americans fleeing slavery confronted the act. Even freeborn African Americans abandoned their homes for the supposed security from oppression that the 49th parallel afforded them.

But not all were willing to acquiesce to the new law that made those in the North "slave catchers of the South." Some of those who were firmly rooted in new communities in the North spoke out against the law or squarely challenged it. Jermain W. Loguen, who escaped from slavery in Tennessee, moved to Syracuse, New York, by 1840 and became a pastor of the African Methodist Episcopal Zion Church and a key agent of the Underground Railroad in that city. At a meeting in Syracuse to discuss enforcement of the law, Loguen encouraged defiance and convinced Syracuse residents to make their city a refuge for fugitives. As for his own intention regarding the law, he declared that he did not fear it. "I will not live a slave. . . . And if force is employed to reenslave me, I shall make preparations to meet the crisis as becomes a man." Samuel Ringgold Ward agreed. The fugitive from Maryland who had become a newspaper editor and minister invoked "the right of Revolution" and argued that the question was "whether a man has a right to himself and his children, his hopes and his happiness, for this world and the world to come." Anyone who sought to abridge that right "need not live at all."[37] Ward's concern for his safety convinced him to leave America for good.

The Fugitive Slave Act of 1850 and the Kansas-Nebraska Act of 1854 were but the opening challenges to the legal standing of African Americans in the decade before the war. By 1857 the Supreme Court decision in the case *Dred Scott v. Sandford* would deny American citizenship to all African Americans, whether freeborn or freed. The case had been filed by antislavery men on behalf of Dred Scott and his family. Scott claimed that he and his wife had been taken to and domiciled in a free state (Illinois) and later had lived in free territory (Wisconsin) and hence should be declared free. The Scott family, which also included two daughters, endured years of litigation, claiming victory in two instances just to see the decisions overturned in higher courts. When their case finally reached the U.S. Supreme Court, a proslavery majority ruled against them. The court declared that African Americans, whether enslaved or free, were not citizens of the United States and hence could not sue in the federal court. In an effort to settle the slavery question for all time, Chief Justice Roger Taney ruled that owners of enslaved laborers had the right to transport and domicile their property wherever they wished. Congress could not restrict this right, even in the territories.[38]

By this time, Lincoln had joined the newly formed Republican Party, which was solidly against slavery's expansion. In speaking out against the *Dred Scott* decision in Springfield in the summer of 1857, he refuted the idea that the Founding Fathers intended to exclude African Americans from the phrase "the people" as it applied to the Declaration of Independence and the Constitution. He agreed with Justice Benjamin Curtis, who in the dissenting opinion in *Dred Scott v. Sandford* argued that since black men were able to vote in five of the original thirteen states at the nation's founding, they were included in the body politic. Lincoln also challenged the argument that supporters of the idea of black inclusion in the Declaration of Independence secretly desired amalgamation. Instead, he asserted, it was slavery that led to racial mixing. Hence, the only logical way to prevent "indiscriminate amalgamation" was to separate the races.

As long as slavery existed, owners would abuse the power they had over their bondwomen. The extension of slavery would simply spread the practice that "nearly all white people" found so abhorrent.[39]

The *Dred Scott* decision stabbed at the heart of the African American desire for equality. It was not just that the Supreme Court's decision opened the door for the expansion of slavery; it denied even free black men and women citizenship in the country of their birth. The reaction to the decision among black people was at once hopeful and sorrow-filled. Some in the African American community took the optimistic view espoused by Frederick Douglass. "My hopes were never brighter than now," Douglass declared. "I have no fear that the national conscience will be put to sleep by such an open, glaring and scandalous tissue of lies as that decision is." African Americans were advised to cast off despondency and see the desperation of the *Dred Scott* decision as evidence that the slave power was weakening and that the principles of freedom would prevail.[40]

But optimism was hardly universal. From Philadelphia, William Still, abolitionist, agent on the Underground Railroad, and correspondent for the Canada-based *Provincial Freeman*, reported that in that city African Americans were not surprised by the decision, but he found that "its influence has been more discouraging and prostrating to the hopes of the colored man, than any preceding act of tyranny ever perpetrated upon him by this nation."[41]

Still's less-than-optimistic view of the future reflected the sentiments of many of those African Americans who were either resident in Canada or affiliated with those who were. H. Ford Douglas, a young abolitionist firebrand who had left Illinois and settled in Chatham, Ontario, for a time, had had enough with speeches and meetings. "Dissolve the Union at once! Put an end to that bogus Government and Constitution," he declared.[42] The editor of the *Provincial Freeman*, Mary Ann Shad Cary, called for the same. "This is not the time for strong words only," she wrote; "when all realize the yoke so forcibly as now why not act? Protests are well enough in their way, but to be of effect, they must point to determined action. Your national ship is rotten, sinking, why not leave it, and why not say so boldly, manfully?"[43]

The *Dred Scott* decision led to unexpected, and sometimes amusing, consequences as individuals took the opportunity to "turn the tables" on those who would deny their humanity. It was a development that Lincoln, with his fondness for humor, would have appreciated. In Marshall, Michigan, a black man was hauled into court and charged with indebtedness. Citing the Supreme Court decision, he declared that he was "not a man, but a mere article of merchandise, and that the court had no jurisdiction of him." Swayed by the logic of his argument, the court amended the plea. In Chicago several fugitives from slavery were arrested and charged with stealing poultry. Their attorney, as in the Michigan case, asked for dismissal of the charges, citing the Supreme Court's ruling that black people were "'*things*,' and not persons, as alleged in the indictment." The state's attorney responded by filing a demurrer, and the judge sustained it, on the grounds that the Supreme Court did not intend its decision to be used in this manner. The accused were brought to trial, but the jury found them "not guilty." And in Bangor, Maine, William Barronett sued David Sands, a black man, for refusing to pay the twenty-dollar debt that the latter owed. Sands argued that since the Supreme Court had declared that African Americans were not citizens of the United States, he could not be sued. The judge accepted his argument, and Sands reportedly left the courtroom "with a smiling face and humming snatches of 'The Devil came fiddling through the town.'"[44]

In the year following the *Dred Scott* decision, Lincoln honed his argument in opposition to the expansion of slavery and availed himself of the opportunities presented to share his views. An extraordinary chance came in the form of a series of seven debates for the Illinois senatorial seat with Democratic incumbent Stephen A. Douglas. Meeting in seven of the state's nine congressional districts (having already spoken in close succession in the two that included Chicago and Springfield), the opponents outlined their interpretation of the intent of the Founding Fathers on the subject of slavery and its extension. Senator Douglas charged Lincoln and the Republicans with being abolitionists and in favor of equality for African Americans. Seeking to reassure fellow Illinoisans that the Republicans had no intention of treading on the rights of Americans, he argued that his party thought slavery morally wrong but recognized the constitutional rights of the slave owner to his or her property. Congress had no authority to touch it where it already existed, but Republicans believed that the national legislature did have the authority to stop its expansion. Lincoln's argument may have comforted moderates, but it only confirmed among staunch abolitionists, including African Americans, that the Republican Party did not embrace their commitment to slavery's demise. Just as unsettling to them was Lincoln's defense against Senator Douglas's insistence that the Republicans sought equality between the races. At Charleston, Lincoln had pleased his audience by declaring that he was "not, nor ever have been in favor of bringing about in any way the social and political equality of the white and black races." He suggested that the physical difference between the two groups would make it impossible for them to ever live as equals. And as long as they occupied the same nation, the white race must hold the superior position.[45]

It was a statement that to the present day allows Lincoln's critics to challenge his commitment to fairness and equal treatment. But in the antiblack environment that was mid-nineteenth century Illinois (and, in general, in the rest of the country as well), Lincoln's words found a willing reception. Although he did not win the senatorial seat, the debates helped to lift him out of obscurity and afforded him recognition as a leader in the still new and evolving Republican Party. This position would benefit him in the coming presidential election, as slavery's future became the central issue.

THE 1860 ELECTION AND
THE LOSS OF UNION

The 1860 presidential campaign revealed the tensions over slavery that permeated both the nation and politics. Not surprisingly, sectional divisions led to the fielding of multiple candidates. Lincoln's old political nemesis, Stephen A. Douglas, represented the "regular" Democratic Party, whose support came primarily from the North. John C. Breckinridge, vice president in the James Buchanan administration, became the candidate of the southern Democrats, who had broken away when the traditional Democratic Party nominated Douglas. The newly formed Constitutional Union Party chose as its standard bearer John Bell, a Tennessee slaveholder who opposed secession. Abraham Lincoln, moderate Republican from Illinois, had won his party's nomination by defeating formidable challengers in William Henry Seward and Salmon P. Chase. But winning the nomination left him far removed from securing the presidency.

Much had transpired since Lincoln had challenged Douglas in the senatorial debates two years earlier. Lincoln had utilized the intervening period to communicate his views on slavery, declaring them in the Midwest and in the East as well. In an Ohio speech he called for a "national policy" that recognized slavery as a wrong and argued that the institution harmed the "general welfare." The solution, he believed, was to prevent slavery's spread into the territories and the free states and to prohibit the reopening of the transatlantic slave trade.[1]

But it was Lincoln's February 27, 1860, address at Cooper Union in New York that would catapult him from a person of regional interest to someone who could command national attention. The invitation to speak had come from James Briggs of the Young Men's Republican Union, a Chase supporter who, it is believed, hoped to weaken the candidacy of Seward by offering up a number of alternative candidates. Originally, Briggs intended Lincoln to speak at Plymouth Church of Brooklyn, where the prominent abolitionist Henry Ward Beecher presided. For reasons unknown, the venue was switched to Cooper Union in Manhattan and, at Lincoln's request, scheduled for February 27.[2]

Lincoln took the occasion at Cooper Union to convey the idea that rather than holding a radical position on slavery, the Republican Party was merely following the intent of the Founding Fathers. It was, in fact, southerners who wished to introduce new concepts that threatened the very Union. He ended his speech with a call to Republicans to remain true to the cause: "Neither let us be slandered from our duty by false accusations against us, nor frightened from it by menaces of destruction to the Government nor of dungeons to ourselves. LET US HAVE FAITH THAT RIGHT MAKES MIGHT, AND IN THAT FAITH, LET US, TO THE END, DARE TO DO OUR DUTY AS WE UNDERSTAND IT."[3] Lincoln covered ground that had been traversed before, but his masterful presentation of the facts and his persuasive argument convinced many in attendance and throughout the North that he was a viable candidate for the presidency.

Lincoln's opponents for the Republican nomination had much to recommend them that was lacking in the former rail-splitter. Both Chase and Seward had executive experience, having served as governors of their respective states. Both had also served in the U.S. Senate. And both men were better known than Lincoln in their advocacy of antislavery. But this also made them vulnerable to those opposed to any hint of radicalism. The Republican Party of 1860 was not inclined to select an abolitionist or anyone who might venture in that direction.

Lincoln was well aware of the difficulty that winning the nomination would entail. In a letter to former Ohio congressman Samuel Galloway in March 1860, he outlined his strategy. Since he was less well known and "not the first choice of a very great many," he suggested that the policy should be to "give no offence to others—leave them in a mood to come to us, if they shall be compelled, to give up their first love." Lincoln also indicated that he did not want to do any "ungenerous thing" to Chase, since the future secretary of the treasury had supported Lincoln in his 1858 run for the U.S. Senate, when other prominent Republicans had declined to back him.[4]

While Cooper Union did not render Lincoln an unchallengeable alternative to Seward and Chase, several factors favored Lincoln's nomination at the 1860 Republican National Convention. Beyond home field advantage—the Chicago location enabled Lincoln as an Illinoisan to enjoy the benefit of "favorite son" status—his moderate stance on slavery recommended him to those who found it difficult (if not impossible) to embrace unconditional abolitionism but who recognized that the institution, unchecked, held the potential to undermine the Union. The party's platform resolved, "The normal condition of all the territory of the United States is that of freedom," and acknowledged the rights of each state "to order and control its own domestic institutions according to its own judgment," which matched Lincoln's views. In addition, Lincoln supporters such as David Davis used their political connections to help secure the votes that he needed. While Seward was favored in the first two ballots, Lincoln (who had finished second in both instances) captured the nomination on the third.[5]

Meanwhile, the Democrats and opponents of the positions of both Democrats and Republicans had met to choose their candidates. The Democratic Convention met in Charleston in late April and immediately became hopelessly divided. The southern wing of the party demanded the adoption of a platform sanctioning slavery in the territories. When the northern Democrats failed to support their position, the southern delegates withdrew from the convention. The remaining delegates were insufficient to give frontrunner Stephen Douglas the two-thirds majority required for nomination; hence, the convention was adjourned. When the Democrats reconvened in Baltimore in June, the two wings of the party decided to meet separately. The northern Democrats nominated Douglas and approved a party platform that resolved to "abide by the decision of the Supreme Court" on matters involving slavery in the territories.[6] The southern delegates nominated Breckinridge and adopted a platform that confirmed the right of all citizens to "settle with their property in the Territory, without their rights . . . being destroyed or impaired by Congressional or Territorial legislation."[7]

Seeking to counter political division and to avoid secession, a group of conservative former Whigs joined with remnants of the Know-Nothings to form the Constitutional Union Party. In their meeting in Baltimore on May 9, the party took no official position on slavery and resolved to "recognize no political principle other than THE CONSTITUTION OF THE COUNTRY, THE UNION OF THE STATES, AND THE ENFORCEMENT OF THE LAWS."[8] Their nominee, John Bell, had enjoyed a long and distinguished political career, having served as a member of both the House of Representatives and the Senate and as Speaker of the House. The wealthy slaveholder opposed the expansion of slavery into the territories and was an ardent supporter of union before the war.

In 1860 few African Americans could vote, but this imposed disability hardly rendered them silent on the parties and their candidates. Although the Republican Party's antislavery stance tended to attract the favorable attention of African Americans, they were reserved in their support for either party. Thomas Hamilton, editor of the *Weekly Anglo-African*, warned his readers that there was little difference between the two parties in terms of end results. "They both entertain the same ideas, and both carry the same burdens," he argued. "The Democratic party would make the white man the master and the black man, the slave," while the Republican Party posed an even greater danger: their professed humanity in the form of banning slavery in the territories was actually a guise for keeping African Americans out. "Their opposition to slavery means opposition to the black man—nothing else." Hamilton cautioned that black people must rely on themselves and the rightness of their cause, not on either the Republicans or the Democrats.[9]

The imperfections of the Republican program convinced H. Ford Douglas that he should not support the presidential candidacy of his fellow Illinoisan. "I know Abraham Lincoln, and I know something about his antislavery," Douglas declared. "I do not believe in the antislavery of Abraham Lincoln, because he is on the side of the slave power." Douglas recalled that two years earlier he had traveled through Illinois in search of Republicans who would be willing to sign a petition supporting the right of black men to testify against white men in court. Lincoln and his friend Senator Lyman Trumbull had declined to support the effort. Douglas believed that no party was worthy of the support of antislavery men if that party was unwilling to secure the rights of citizenship for black men. "I care nothing about that antislavery which wants to make the territories free, while it is unwilling to extend to me, as a man, in the free states, all the rights of a man."[10]

The usually cynical Frederick Douglass was a bit more hopeful in his assessment of the Republican Party and its candidate. While he acknowledged the party's limitations, especially its failure to commit to ending slavery, he nonetheless encouraged black support as it was the best of the options available. "While I see . . . the Republican party is far from an abolition party," he reasoned, "I cannot fail to see also that the Republican party carries with it the anti-slavery sentiment of the North, and that a victory gained by it in the present canvass will be a victory gained by that sentiment over the wickedly aggressive pro-slavery sentiment of the country."[11] And in Lincoln, Douglass initially saw "a man of unblemished private character . . . a cool, well balanced head; great firmness of will; is perseveringly industrious, and one of the most frank, honest men in political life."[12] That view would change after the election, as the president's effort to hold the border states in the Union clashed with the former bondman's insistence on the immediate destruction of slavery.

Lincoln appeared on the ballot of only one of the eleven states destined to secede from the Union in the winter of 1860 and the spring of 1861. He carried none. Lincoln won roughly 40 percent of the popular vote but more than 59 percent of votes in the electoral college, while his old rival Stephen A. Douglas garnered the second highest number of popular votes but finished last in electoral votes.[13] The slavery issue had exacerbated sectionalism, seemingly beyond repair.

The electoral result was too much for South Carolina to abide. On December 20, 1860, the state, in convention, voted an Ordinance of Secession. A subsequent "Declaration of Immediate Causes" (drawn up on December 24) cited grounds for the state's actions. Indicating "frequent violations of the Constitution of the United States by the Federal Government, and its encroachments upon the reserved rights of the States," the declaration identified fourteen northern states that South Carolina claimed had "deliberately broken and disregarded" the compact that fugitives from slavery be returned to their owners. As a consequence, it reasoned, the state was thus released from its obligation to the Union.[14]

Before Lincoln could take office, six additional states had found justification for secession, most of them citing an imminent attack on slavery. In Mississippi, for instance, delegates to the secession convention declared emphatically, "Our position is thoroughly identified with the institution of slavery—the greatest material interest of the world." The only solution to protecting this peculiar property was, they argued, to "secede from the Union framed by our fathers, to secure this as well as every other species of property."[15] While other issues were raised, the overriding one involved the desire to protect slavery.

From the perspective of the seceding states, their concerns were justified. Just one year earlier, in October 1859, abolitionist John Brown had led an attack on the federal arsenal at Harpers Ferry, Virginia, in an effort to arm enslaved men and strike a blow for black freedom. Federal forces under the command of then colonel Robert E. Lee quelled the assault, and John Brown and his men (except five who escaped) were killed outright or executed after conviction. The South saw in this attack a serious challenge to slavery. The incident convinced southerners that northerners would not rest until the institution was destroyed. So when an antislavery Republican seized the presidency, it did not matter that his views on the institution were moderate or that he believed that slavery could not be touched in those states where it already existed.[16]

Lincoln's predecessor, James Buchanan, had taken the least confrontational stance in the secession crisis. He chose to pass his remaining weeks in office ignoring the legal and political challenges

attending a divided nation. Lincoln did not have the luxury of waiting for someone else to solve the problem. Within weeks of his election and the secession of seven states, he privately conveyed his ideas
about national union and black freedom.

Timing was critical, since talks were already underway in Congress that sought a resolution to the secession crisis. In the Senate,
the Committee of Thirteen met on December 18, 1860, to consider
"a plan of adjustment" that would stay the crisis. No fewer than
five compromises were proposed, all of them attempting to protect
slavery where it already existed or pressing for the right to extend it
wherever the slaveholder so desired. The Crittenden Compromise,
authored by Senator John Crittenden of Kentucky, was one of the
more comprehensive. Crittenden's proposal called for the adoption of
six constitutional amendments and four resolutions designed to allay
the fears of southerners and avert universal secession. The measures
were overwhelmingly pro-South: slavery would be protected in the
current slaveholding states in perpetuity; the territories south of the
Missouri Compromise line extending westward would be opened to
slavery; Congress could not touch slavery in the District of Columbia
without the consent and compensation of the owners and as long as
it continued to exist in Maryland and Virginia; and the federal government would be required to compensate owners who lost human
property because of interference on the part of free jurisdictions. In
an extraordinary move, Crittenden proposed that Congress be prohibited from instituting any future amendment that would counter
these measures or permit interference with slavery in the slave states.
Not surprisingly, both the Senate and the House of Representatives
rejected the compromise.[17]

The Crittenden Compromise found Lincoln willing to concede
(in part) the issue of enforcement of the Fugitive Slave Act, but he
was emphatically unwilling to embrace the idea of slavery's extension. In a series of letters to Republican leaders, he held steadfastly
to his position. "Let there be no compromise on the question of
extending slavery," he wrote to Senator Trumbull. "If there be, all
our labor is lost, and, ere long, must be done again. The dangerous
ground—that into which some of our friends have a hankering to

run—is Pop[ular] Sov[ereignty]. Have none of it. Stand firm. The tug has to come, & better now, than any time hereafter."[18] As members of the House and the Senate debated the "fix" that could come from a constitutional amendment, Lincoln let it be known that he did not favor such action but declared his support for "the maintenance inviolate of the rights of the States, and especially the right of each state to order and control its own domestic institutions according to its own judgment exclusively."[19]

As he waited to leave Springfield for Washington, Lincoln's commitment to nonextension only grew. "On the territorial question—that is, the question of extending slavery under the national auspices,—I am inflexible," he wrote to secretary of state designate William H. Seward. "I am for no compromise which *assists* or *permits* the extension of the institution on soil owned by the nation. And any trick by which the nation is to acquire territory, and then allow some local authority to spread slavery over it, is as obnoxious as any other. I take it that to effect some such result as this, and to put us again on the high-road to a slave empire is the object of all these proposed compromises. I am against it."[20]

In the meantime, two efforts were underway in Washington to prevent the secession of additional states. The Peace Conference, proposed by Virginia and led by former president John Tyler of that state, met on February 4 and drew 131 delegates from twenty-one states. The three-week-long meeting essentially adopted the provisions of the Crittenden Compromise and suffered the same fate as that earlier effort. Those delegates in attendance had arrived with the aim in mind less to compromise than to hold firm to their respective parties' ideology. In a time of crisis, such behavior was doomed to failure. The second effort was initiated by Ohio congressman Thomas Corwin, who proposed a thirteenth amendment that would simply assure the South that "no amendment shall be made to the Constitution which will authorize or give to Congress the power to abolish or interfere, within any state, with the domestic institutions thereof, including that of persons held to labor or service by the laws of said states." The proposed amendment passed both houses of Congress, by a vote of 133–65 in the House on February 28 and 24–12 in the Senate on March 2. In keeping with his obligation as president, Lincoln forwarded it to the states for ratification on March 16, not quite two weeks after he took the oath of office. In the weeks that followed before the start of the war, only two states—Ohio and Maryland—completed ratification.[21] After the attack on Fort Sumter, the ratification process ceased.

When Lincoln delivered his inaugural address two days after the proposed amendment passed the Senate, he alluded to the measure and declared that as it was "implied constitutional law," he had "no objections to it being made express and irrevocable." While he did not officially endorse or discourage ratification, he doubtless was satisfied that the measure did not violate his own views on slaveholders' rights in the states. In fact, in his address to the American people on March 4, he had expended considerable effort to explain his position on slavery. Given the unfolding crisis, his remarks were eagerly anticipated. For the most part, he reiterated what he had privately declared as president-elect. He began by attempting to reassure the slaveholding states that they should not fear that a Republican administration would do harm to them or to their property. He declared that he had neither the authority nor the inclination to touch slavery and assured them that "all the protection which, consistently with the Constitution and the laws, can be given will be cheerfully given to all the States." But despite his conciliatory tone, Lincoln did not yield on the idea of an indissoluble Union. "The Union is unbroken," he declared, and had the right to "constitutionally defend, and maintain itself." There was no need for violence and bloodshed, unless the federal government was compelled to do so in its effort to "hold, occupy, and possess the property, and places belonging to the government, and to collect the duties and imposts."[22]

Lincoln's words gave comfort to some and disappointed others. Nothing he could have said, short of agreeing with the South's position that they had the right and were justified in seceding, would have been sufficient to calm their anxiety over the election of a Republican administration. His address met their expectations. In the soon-to-secede state of Virginia, the *Richmond Enquirer* saw his remarks as a "declaration of war." "Mr. Lincoln's Inaugural Address is before our readers—couched in the cool, unimpassioned, deliberate language of the fanatic, with the purpose of pursuing the promptings of fanaticism even to the dismemberment of the Government with the horrors of civil war," it proclaimed. The *Charleston Mercury* responded in similar fashion: "If ignorance could add anything to folly, or insolence to brutality, the president of the Northern States of America has, in this address, achieved it. A more lamentable display of feeble inability to grasp the circumstances of this momentous emergency, could scarcely have been exhibited." While the South appeared to be solidly critical of the address, northern reactions were mixed, often reflecting party affiliation. In a close review of Lincoln's remarks, the *New York Herald* (a strong supporter of the Democrats) found the new president to be confused and unable to determine which path the nation should take. "Not a single pledge or proposition with regard to the future, is contained in the Inaugural Message, from beginning to end," the editorial suggested. "It is neither candid nor statesmanlike, nor does it possess any essential of dignity or patriotism. It would have caused a Washington to mourn, and would have inspired Jefferson, Madison, or Jackson with contempt." But the *Philadelphia Inquirer* heard differently. The president's message was "in admirable tone and temper." The editor praised Lincoln for his sincerity and for his desire to allay the fears of the southern people. Here was a man who simply wanted to do what was right.[23]

For the most part, Lincoln's address left African Americans unimpressed and frustrated. His assurances to the seceded states dashed black expectations and invited unbridled indictment. Leading the way, as usual, Frederick Douglass charged that the president missed the occasion to condemn the secessionists and their inhuman economic system. "Some thought that we had in Mr. Lincoln the nerve and decision of an Oliver Cromwell," Douglass wrote, "but the result shows that we merely have a continuation of the Pierces and Buchanans, and that the Republican President bends the knee to slavery as readily as any of his infamous predecessors." Rather than take the manly position of rebuking the southerners for their "barbarous system of robbery," the president had sought to conciliate traitors by convincing them of "what an excellent slave hound he is, and how he regards the right to recapture fugitive slaves a constitutional duty." The *Weekly Anglo-African* posed to its readers the question, "What hope does President Lincoln's Inaugural hold for us?" The answer, apparently, was nothing positive. The editor lamented that Lincoln's honesty and straightforward language left little doubt of his intentions. Alluding to his pledge to enforce the Fugitive Slave Act, the paper chided him for his willingness to serve as "National Kidnapper." Although African Americans found some assurance in Lincoln's call for the safeguarding of the rights of free black men and women, lest they be taken up as fugitives, that was not enough to soothe the sting that enforcement of the Fugitive Slave Act delivered.[24]

For African Americans, the issue was less about preserving the Union than about slavery, and they feared that the North would seek to keep the nation together by sacrificing the well-being of black people. Slavery was the disease, and only its eradication could heal America. They derided the timidity with which northerners greeted southern secession, their fear silencing them to the audacity of the slaveholding states. "The attitude of the Northern people in this crisis will crimson the cheeks of their children's children with shame," Douglass predicted. "The arrogance and impudence of the traitors are only exceeded by the sneaking cowardice and pitiful imbecility of the Government, and of the Northern people, who, by mobbing down freedom of speech, crying 'no coercion,' and whining for compromise, prove themselves of a piece with the Government." Douglass and his compatriots were decidedly against compromise with the rebels, even to preserve the Union. "If there is not wisdom and virtue enough in the land to rid the country of slavery," he argued, "then the next best thing is to let the South go to her own place, and be made to drink the wine cup of wrath and fire, which her long career of cruelty, barbarism and blood shall call down upon her guilty head."[25]

African Americans occupied a unique position in the disunion drama and the ensuing debate. Anticipating that open conflict between white men would inevitably benefit black people, they greeted disunion with cautious optimism. Doubtless, many shared H. Ford Douglas's sentiment that secessionists should "stand not upon the order of your going, but go at once."[26] Some, however, feared that the removal of federal restraints could result in a more robust institution that would inflict even greater oppression on its victims. The *Weekly Anglo-African*'s editor, Thomas Hamilton, sounded a cautionary note. He warned of the potential reopening of the international slave trade and the probable insurrection that great numbers and more severe repression might produce. In the instance of a slave uprising, he wondered, would the federal government feel compelled to intervene on the side of the slave owners, even though they had severed their ties with the nation?[27] Hamilton's question would be answered in time.

WAR, UNION, AND SLAVERY

Lincoln had taken the presidential oath of office with his antislavery credentials intact, but a conversion to the idea of immediate abolitionism (at least publicly stated) was nearly two years away. A protracted war that tested the ability of the North to defeat the secessionists would ultimately lead the president to use whatever means at his disposal to attack the institution at the center of the conflict. But for now, he would consistently convey to both Unionists and Confederates that the South's domestic institution was safe.

The Fort Sumter crisis less than two months into Lincoln's presidency tested his commitment to a policy of appeasement and conciliation. Until now, the government had not acted with force to protect federal installations that were located in Confederate territory. Fort Sumter, in Charleston Harbor, presented an immediate crisis because it was running out of food. Lincoln's decision to provision the fort was met with bombardment by Confederate batteries. The president's response was to call on the state militias to put down the revolt and enforce the laws. The goal was to secure seventy-five thousand men for the task. As he prepared for war, he gave assurances that he intended no harm to the person or property of "peaceful citizens."[1]

The northern people responded enthusiastically to Lincoln's call, certain that the war would be of short duration and that their just cause and superior resources would ensure Union victory. The free states complied quickly and had little difficulty reaching their quota. But sentiment was not uniform in the North. The *New York Herald* saw the North and South headed toward an escalation of hostilities and urged the residents of the city to "make a solemn and imposing effort in behalf of peace." Indiana's conservative *Weekly Vincennes Western Sun* believed that northern military action had to be justified by explicit southern hostility. The paper declared that although it did not support Lincoln's response to Fort Sumter, "if matters progress further—if the south commits any overt act against the Government we will not be one to sustain her." The liberal *Vincennes Gazette* thought the *Sun*'s position was preposterous. "Will you be so patriotic as to inform us what 'overt action' you are awaiting?" it asked. "The South seizes the forts and you are mute; the South takes possession of Government property—you are dumb; the South steals the contents of the New Orleans Mint—you have not a word to say; the South fires upon a vessel with the national flag, the glorious stars and stripes, and you are as the 'sheep before the shearer.' . . . If trampling under foot the Constitution, destroying the union, Levying war against the Government, and defying the laws are not overt acts, then God help us."[2]

The Upper South states did not see it that way. Rather than rally to the federal cause, Virginia, North Carolina, Arkansas, and Tennessee declined to send troops. Instead, they voted ordinances of secession and joined their compatriots in the Confederacy. The response of the remaining border states—Kentucky, Missouri, Maryland, and Delaware—was less dramatic but worrisome to the Lincoln administration nonetheless. Governors initially refused to provide troops, and the loyalty of these states to the Union remained a source of concern for Lincoln for much of the war. Nearly surrounding the federal capital, Maryland proved especially dangerous as some of its Confederate sympathizing residents aided the rebel government with impunity.

If most northerners supported the cause of union, African Americans found hope for their own cause in the commencement of war. The *Weekly Anglo-African* embraced armed conflict as "another step in the drama of American Progress," a movement toward liberty. "God speed the conflict," it declared. "May the cup be drained to the dregs, for only then can this nation of sluggards know the disease and its remedy." Special scorn was heaped upon Virginia. The state represented for many, especially African Americans, the establishment and development of slavery in America. "Thank God, the hour of retribution has come," wrote one enthusiastic supporter of the war. "Virginia! Mother of Harlots—Plunderer of Cradles . . . Butcher—Pirate—Kidnapper—Slaveocrat—the murderer of John Brown and his gallant band—at last will meet her just doom. . . . God speed the punishment!"[3]

African American men wasted little time in offering their services to help deliver the sentence. Black leaders urged their brothers to join the cause that would surely lead to the destruction of slavery. George Lawrence, new editor of the *Weekly Anglo-African*, remarked facetiously that five thousand black men, organized as guerrilla units and deployed through the Virginia, Kentucky, and Tennessee mountains and the coastal swamps, could make quick work of the rebellion. "We want Nat Turner—not speeches; Denmark Vesey—not resolutions; John Brown—not meetings."[4]

Throughout the North, black men formed drill companies in preparation for being called to service. But the North, generally, was not yet interested in attacking slavery or in bringing black men into what most northerners saw as a "white man's war." When black men in New York attempted to meet and offer their services to the government, the local police refused them the right of assembly on the grounds that "it might lead to some unpleasantness in New York, as well as exasperate the South." Similar incidents occurred in other northern communities.[5]

In addition to wishing not to offend southern sensibilities, northern objections to black men serving as soldiers resulted from long-held attitudes about black inferiority and cowardice. Frederick Douglass attempted to dispel such views by reminding Americans of the valiant effort of black soldiers in previous wars. "That [African Americans] are not largely represented in the loyal army, is the fault of the Government. . . . They were good enough to help win American independence but they are not good enough to help preserve that independence against treason and rebellion."[6] Rejected by the government, black men nonetheless prepared for that time when necessity would erode the North's resolve to deny them the opportunity to fight.

Despite the desire among many black men to render military service, support for the Union was hardly unconditional. African Americans let it be known that their participation was contingent upon the government's willingness to end slavery. Advocates for freedom were reminded that the North was not committed to the liberation of the enslaved and that Lincoln himself had declared noninterference with southern slavery. Until such commitment was secured, they were told, the "patriotically inclined" should "keep their blood for a better market than that in which Old Abe and Ben Butler keep stalls."[7] As Americans they honored the flag, but they had no obligation to fight under it until the nation acknowledged the rightness of the *African* American cause. "Emancipation or Extermination!," the motto of the John Brown abolitionists, became the rallying cry for those who disagreed with the idea that they should "fight *for* the government." Instead, they asserted, it was their duty to "aid in making the slaves free." Moreover, northern black men demanded that they be granted the same rights as white men. "Until then," they declared, "we are in no condition to fight under the flag which gives us no protection."[8] Perhaps B. K. Sampson, a young black orator from Ohio, put it best. At a rally in Cleveland, he declared, "The presumption is that we exercise unfaltering devotion to the Union; but our patriotism and our hopes arise not from the efforts of McClellan nor the Administration. . . . My highest ambition is to strike a death blow to slavery. . . . We would fight for more than country, for more than a union of states; we would defend more than human laws, we would defend those which are divine. . . . That is a noble soul who would lay his life upon the altar of his country, but nobler far is he who dies to free his brother man."[9]

If at the start of the war, Lincoln and northerners were not inclined to make the conflict about black freedom or to accept African American offers of assistance, an escalation of the conflict forced a reassessment. Before the year had ended, the president and Congress would come to understand the advantage that four million people "held to labor" gave to the secessionist forces and how that same force could benefit the Union.

The seeds of change began to germinate at a little stretch of land known to the victors of this first major battle of the war as Manassas and to the vanquished as Bull Run. The battle cured Lincoln and northerners of the belief that the war would be swift or that the secessionists could be either coaxed or forced back into the national fold through peaceful means. The armies had engaged each other previously, but the results had been, for the most part, inconclusive. Bull Run was significant not only for the decisiveness of the Confederate victory but also because northern civilians were on hand to witness the spectacular defeat. By mid-July, mindful that the term of service for the ninety-day volunteers was about to expire, Lincoln had pressed Union forces to attack. Thirty miles south of the District of Columbia lay the community of Manassas and the nearby creek known as Bull Run. On the morning of July 21, residents of the federal city, picnic baskets in hand, went out to the site where overconfident and inexperienced Union troops had moved into position to engage the secessionist forces. The ensuing rout saw federals retreating from the Confederate advance as civilian spectators fled for their lives.[10]

An unintended (but hardly unexpected) consequence of the First Battle of Bull Run was the attachment of fugitives from slavery to the retreating Union army. Months before, enslaved African Americans had taken advantage of the unsettled conditions created by secession to flee to Union-held forts, where they hoped to receive asylum with President Lincoln's soldiers. Their confidence in finding protection prompted Frederick Douglass to declare, "It is more than probable that [the slaves] have given Mr. Lincoln credit for having intentions towards them far more benevolent and just than any he is known to cherish. . . . His pledges to protect and uphold slavery in the States have not reached them, while certain dim, undefined, but large and exaggerated notions of his emancipating purposes have taken firm hold of them, and have grown larger and firmer with every look, nod and undertone of their oppressors."[11]

As early as March 1861, fugitives had arrived at Fort Pickens, near Pensacola, Florida, guided by the belief that they could find asylum with the federal forces still in possession of the military installation.[12] In the absence of any specific guidelines to inform their decisions regarding return of the property of rebels, commanders faced with the problem of black flight often drew on the president's inaugural pledge to uphold the Fugitive Slave Act of 1850. At Fort Pickens, the fugitives were swiftly returned to their owners. Once hostilities commenced, others descended on federal posts with varying degrees of success. At Fortress Monroe, Virginia, commanding general Benjamin F. Butler helped to shape wartime policy regarding fugitives by admitting Frank Baker, Shepard Mallory, and James Townsend to the fort. The three men had arrived on May 23, 1861, one day after Butler had taken command. Declaring that they were the property of one Charles K. Mallory, a Confederate colonel, they claimed to have run away because their owner intended to transport them to North Carolina where they would be put to labor for the secessionist forces. Butler obliged, declining to return them to Mallory. Instead, he treated them as confiscated property, declaring them "contraband-of-war" and putting them to work as military laborers.[13] Through "the mysterious spiritual telegraph, which runs through the slave population," others learned of the favorable reception enjoyed by Baker, Mallory, and Townsend, and in a few days fugitives were fleeing to the "freedom fort." Edward L. Pierce, who was later assigned to organize the contrabands in the area, reported that "on Sunday morning, May 26th, eight negroes stood before the quarters of General Butler, waiting for an audience. . . . On May 27th, forty-seven negroes of both sexes and all ages, from three months to eighty-five years, among whom were half a dozen entire families, came in one squad. Another lot of a dozen good field-hands arrived the same day; and then they continued to come by twenties, thirties, and forties."[14] By the end of July, the numbers had reached nine hundred.

Fugitives from slavery proved problematic for a president who was trying to coax secessionists back into the Union through appeasement while struggling to maintain the loyalty of nonsecessionist slaveholders. His troubles extended beyond the Confederacy, as the enslaved laborers of Maryland planters sought freedom as well. Maryland congressional representative Charles Calvert appealed directly to the president for relief in securing his constituents' property. Referring to the "untiring efforts of the Union men" in his state to support the northern cause, Calvert now asked Lincoln to do something for them. Since the stationing of voluntary forces in and around the District of Columbia, Maryland planters had experienced a continuing loss of their laborers who escaped to the camps. Here they found sanctuary and employment with the Union army, despite Maryland's Unionist status. When the soldiers left the area, they often permitted the fugitives to come along. Some of them managed to flee from Maryland altogether, finding new homes in Union-occupied northern Virginia. Calvert warned that a continuation of such practices would produce great animosity against the government. He urged Lincoln to instruct commanders of these encampments to ban all enslaved people from them and to confine those already there until their owners could recapture them. Ever mindful of the tenuous loyalty of the border states, Lincoln inquired of the general-in-chief, Winfield Scott, if it might be possible to allow the owners to retrieve their property. The sensitive nature of the matter prompted the president to ask that his inquiry be kept confidential.[15]

The pledge Lincoln had made to recognize the rights of slaveholders was hard enough for abolitionists to accept; actual enforcement of the Fugitive Slave Act by Union soldiers rankled those committed to black freedom even more. "[T]he Union refuses to let white men sell the Southerners food," J. Sella Martin, himself a prewar fugitive from slavery, argued, "and yet they return slaves to work on the plantations to raise all the food that the Southerners want. They arrest traitors, and yet make enemies of the colored people, North and South; and if they do force the slave to fight for his master, as the only hope of being benefited by the war, they may thank their own cowardice and prejudice for the revenge of the negro's aim and the retribution of his bullet while fighting against them in the Southern States."[16]

Standing the idea of enslaved people as property on its head, Frederick Douglass argued that legally they had no more standing than livestock, farm equipment, and lands. "The right to a slave is no more sacred than the right to a horse or cow, or a barrel of flour," Douglass protested. He wondered why the property of the nonslaveholding Richmond merchant was subject to seizure and appropriation while enslaved men and women whose owners had helped to bring on the rebellion were returned and treated like "property too sacred to lose its character as property, even though its owner is an open traitor to the Government."[17] Douglass warned, as did Martin, that the government's actions would make enemies of those who could be made allies.

Others questioned whether the war was even defensible without the destruction of slavery as a focus. Orson S. Murray, who had spent much of his life in the service of antislavery, believed that "no war is justifiable, except for freedom." Murray expressed profound disappointment that the government had not given any indication that it intended to move in that direction. "This war has no word, no act, for freedom," he complained. "It is all for slavery. The Government is for slavery."[18]

Prominent Republicans, concerned that the president was overlooking the most obvious solution to putting down the rebellion, called on him and stated their case. Within days of the Bull Run defeat, Senators Charles Sumner and Zachariah Chandler of Massachusetts and Michigan, respectively, visited the president and urged him to expand the war's aim to include emancipation as a military necessity. The resulting chaos, they believed, would bring the Confederacy to its knees. Lincoln did not deny the truth of their assertions but declined to follow their advice since such action, he believed, would not be supported by current northern sentiment.[19]

The advantage that enslaved laborers gave to the Confederacy doubtless influenced the actions of Congress in early August. Understanding that every black orderly, cook, teamster, blacksmith, or builder of defenses benefited the secessionists, as such labor enabled white men to concentrate on soldiering, Congress in August 1861 passed the First Confiscation Act, which allowed for the seizure of property (including enslaved laborers) used to aid the revolt against the government. Generally, support for or opposition to the measure followed region and party affiliation, with Democrats and border state representatives opposing it and Republicans casting a vote in its favor. Lincoln signed the bill but did so reluctantly, doubtless believing that this escalated the conflict rather than suppressed it and because he was still working through his options in regard to dealing with slavery.[20]

Three weeks later General John C. Frémont, commander of the Department of the West, gave the president even greater cause for concern when Frémont declared the enslaved property of disloyal owners in Union Missouri free. Worried that such action would "alarm our Southern Union friends, and turn them against us—perhaps ruin our rather fair prospect for Kentucky," Lincoln asked the general to bring the decree into conformity with the First Confiscation Act. When Frémont refused to act on his own accord, replying that the president would have to "openly direct me to make the concession," Lincoln sent a second letter ordering him to comply.[21]

Responses to the president's rejection of Frémont's emancipating efforts came swiftly and forcefully. Henry Jones, a "citisen of Connecticut," assured Lincoln that "a chord has been touched in the hearts of brave and true men that will vibrate through out the length and breadth of the land." He suggested that Lincoln's actions would unify those men who heretofore had not been certain of the president's policy regarding slavery. He and they were now prepared to welcome the president as a Democrat whose "adhearence to the constitution and laws of the land will soon bring the nation out of this great trouble."[22] Sixty-five-year-old William Prince sought to assure Lincoln that he had "adopted the only fair conservative course" in his order to Frémont. The fanatics would object, he predicted, but "all honest & honorable men will approve your consistent, prudent, & just course."[23]

But for every letter from a supporter, there were many dissenting voices that objected strenuously to the Frémont incident. For Charles Reed, an acquaintance from Lincoln's days in the Illinois legislature, the president's order had "produced the deepest sadness and consternation." Furthermore, he blamed the order for the downturn in the number of men volunteering to join the Union army.[24] The citizens of Coldwater, Michigan, responded similarly. Meeting at the local courthouse, they drew up resolutions in support of Frémont's proclamation and condemned Lincoln's response. The proclamation, they argued, was "demanded by sound wisdom and an imperious necessity" in that it sought to protect the "union loving" residents of Missouri who were subject to abuse from the rebels. The citizens of

Coldwater informed Lincoln that the government's attitude in regard to slavery "weakens and jeopardizes the loyal cause."[25]

Speaking on behalf of its subscribers and other African Americans throughout the North, the *Christian Recorder* reported the "considerable dissatisfaction" that was felt when Lincoln rescinded Frémont's proclamation. "The country rejoiced when they heard of the bold act of the commander of the Western Division, for it was felt to be an effective blow at the very heart of the present wicked rebellion." The newspaper found it "greatly to be regretted that the President has thought it necessary to check the order of the western leader, and to confine him to the mere letter of the Act of Confiscation." It predicted that Lincoln's actions would "dishearten the nation" and lead to loss of support from those who heretofore had enthusiastically come to the aid of the government.[26] Douglass judged this the worst of the administration's numerous poorly considered actions. "Instead of standing by the General, and approving his energetic conduct, they have humbled and crippled him in the presence of his enemies."[27]

Frémont supporters expressed concern that the president might force the general to give up his command or, at the very least, encourage him to resign. A well-meaning, self-styled "plain business man" wrote to Lincoln to offer an unsolicited character reference for the embattled general. Charles S. Homer's endorsement was prefaced by the acknowledgment that Homer had suffered serious financial loss as a result of prior business dealings with Frémont. Yet Homer found him to be "courteous—humane—cautious—energetic—truthful—brave! Resembling Joan of Arc—an enthusiast in all things;—like her Genl. Frémont should be made serviceable to his country." He would "not trust Gen. Frémont with money" but would "follow his fortunes in the field and there . . . aid him with money, or with blood."[28]

Douglass was also concerned that Frémont might lose his command, but his response was to sound an ominous warning: "If Government shall humble merit, and exalt imbecility, displace Generals who are a terror to the rebels, and promote those who excite no alarm . . . it would not be strange if the patience of the people should entirely break down, and if some determined man of military genius should rise out of the social chaos, and displace the civil power altogether."[29]

Lincoln chose to ignore many of the attacks arising from the Fré-mont affair, but the one penned by Illinois senator Orville H. Brown-ing demanded an unflinching response. Shortly after the president checked Frémont's attempt at emancipation, Browning had written a letter that suggested that Lincoln's order "disheartens our friends, and represses their ardor." Hinting, doubtless, at Lincoln's preoc-cupation with securing the support of the border states, Browning complained that "measures are sometimes shaped too much with a view to satisfy men of doubtful loyalty, instead of the true friends of the Country. There has been too much tenderness towards traitors and rebels."[30] Lincoln's response to his old friend was blunt. "Yours of the 17th is just received; and coming from you, I confess it astonishes me," he wrote. "Genl. Frémont's proclamation, as to confiscation of property, and the liberation of slaves, is *purely political*, and not within the range of *military* law, or necessity. . . . If the General needs them, he can seize them, and use them; but when the need is past, it is not for him to fix their permanent future condition. . . . I cannot assume this reckless position; nor allow others to assume it on my responsibility."[31]

One may never know the impact that the tension over the Fré-mont order had on Lincoln. In any case, by the fall of 1861, he was prepared to confront the problem of slavery on his own terms. His plan involved weakening the resolve of the Confederacy by facilitat-ing the irrevocable separation of the border states from those that had already seceded. As early as November 1861, the president had begun devising a plan to persuade Delaware to free the roughly two thousand enslaved men and women who still resided within its borders. Lincoln drafted two proposed laws that would call for gradual abolition with compensation to the owners paid by the fed-eral government. The primary difference between the two proposals was in the length of time allowed for emancipation to take place; years versus decades separated the two. The first proposal called for incremental emancipation, with specific groups acquiring their freedom according to age and with slavery eradicated by 1867. The second proposed a more gradual emancipation, with freedom com-ing immediately to anyone born after the law went into effect or to those who were already thirty-five or older. The remainder would be freed on the attainment of thirty-five years. The process would be completed by 1893. Both proposals suggested apprenticeship for children until age twenty-one and eighteen for males and females, respectively.[32] To the president's disappointment, Delaware favored neither proposal and declined to embrace his efforts.

Despite the steadfast resolve of the slaveholders to retain their property, public opinion was shifting on a related issue: international slave trading. In 1807 the nation had outlawed the trade for its citizens (effective January 1, 1808) and later created the African Squadron, which, in collaboration with Great Britain, policed the waters along the west coast of Africa in an effort to suppress the trade. The small fleet of American vessels proved inadequate for the task, though, and, in comparison to the British effort, it seized few ships that had violated the law.[33]

In the midst of the crisis over slavery's expansion, a movement had surfaced that aimed at reopening the international slave trade to the United States. An influx of enslaved laborers, proponents believed, would help to counter threats to the institution. Most southerners realized, however, that getting the free states to agree to such action would be impossible. In the meantime, southern planters benefited from the continuing illegal trade that served the needs primarily of those in Brazil and Cuba but that also kept the pipeline open to the slaveholding American South.

Although the war resulted in an even smaller American presence along the African coast, the effort to suppress smuggling persisted. In the winter of 1862, the northern people witnessed the seriousness of the Lincoln administration's commitment to enforcing the law. Thirty-six-year-old Nathaniel Gordon, the captain of the slaver *Erie*, had been convicted and condemned under a forty-year-old law that had declared the international slave trade to be piracy, with death imposed upon conviction. Heretofore, no American had suffered the ultimate punishment for this crime, and Gordon had every reason to believe that his experience would be no different. A native of Portland, Maine, he allegedly had engaged in at least three earlier voyages to acquire human cargo. When the crewmen of the U.S.

steamer *Mohican* encountered the *Erie* on the West African coast and boarded it on August 8, 1860, they discovered nearly nine hundred enslaved men, women, and children, from infants to those up to forty years old. Gordon appealed to Lincoln for clemency, and thousands of sympathizers signed petitions in support of commutation of the death sentence.[34] Attempts to influence the decision of the president came from opponents of clemency as well. Lincoln had preferred to commute the sentence and have the slave trader live out his days in confinement while reflecting on his terrible misdeeds. But he felt that "justice and the majesty of law" demanded that there be "at least one specific instance, of a professional slave-trader, a Northern white man, given the exact penalty of death because of the incalculable number of deaths he and his kind inflicted upon black men amid the horror of the sea-voyage from Africa."[35] All Lincoln chose to offer the condemned man was a two-week stay, just enough time for Gordon to make "the necessary preparation for the awful change which awaits him."[36] On February 21, 1862, Gordon was hanged, earning him the dubious distinction of being the first and only American to be executed for such a crime.

The African American community received the news of Gordon's execution with satisfaction and praised Lincoln's refusal to commute the man's sentence. "The firmness of President Lincoln in this affair is the most solid indication of character he has yet manifested," offered the *Weekly Anglo-African*. "Whatever in the coming hours, he may do to put down slavery, it is enough for the present that he has planted his broad foot squarely down upon the slave-trade; he need not move that foot, but only heft it a little more, and slavery already pale and trembling and laboring under self-induced convulsion will be squelched out also. God give him the grace, and keep away Kentucky advisers from him."[37]

In March, perhaps sensing that the North was losing patience with his deference to the slaveholding border states, Lincoln sent a message to Congress recommending that it support by "pecuniary aid" any state willing to implement a gradual abolition of slavery. Lincoln reasoned that if the slaveholding Union states removed the connection that bound them to the Confederacy, the latter would be forced to give up any expectation that it would ever grow larger.[38] One month later, Congress responded to the president's proposal by legislating funds to assist with gradual, compensated emancipation.

The spring and summer of 1862 proved especially busy for a Congress willing to address matters of slavery and freedom. Despite the accepted practice of admitting runaways into the Union lines, commanders in the field continued to allow their own personal views to shape their responses. Hence, on March 13, in an effort to legislate official policy and ensure uniformity, Congress prohibited military personnel from assisting in the return of runaways to their owners.[39] Any officer found guilty of violating the law would be dismissed from the service.

Congress also exercised its authority over the territories and the District of Columbia to outlaw slavery in those jurisdictions. The District of Columbia Emancipation Bill, introduced in December 1861 by Massachusetts abolitionist Senator Henry Wilson, stipulated "that all persons held to service or labor within the District of Columbia by reason of African descent are hereby discharged and freed of and from all claim to such service or labor."[40] The president was authorized to appoint three commissioners to investigate every claim and appraise the value of each enslaved person. Congress had appropriated one million dollars to carry out the emancipation plan; compensation was not to exceed three hundred dollars, to be paid to those owners who could take the loyalty oath. An additional one hundred thousand dollars had been allocated to facilitate the "voluntary" colonization of the men and women thus freed by the act's provisions.[41]

Congress passed the District of Columbia Emancipation Bill on Friday, April 11, over the objections of those who doubted the constitutionality of the government seizing private property without adequate compensation. District residents also lacked the authority to make their own laws or to offer any sustained or meaningful opposition to unpopular measures proposed by Congress. Despite the relatively insignificant population of enslaved persons in the city—at the time of Lincoln's inauguration, 3,100 among a black population of 14,000 and a total of 75,000—District residents had not supported emancipation. But the city's designation as a federal enclave meant that Congress could ignore the residents' preferences on the matter. And it did.

The bill reached the president on Monday, April 14, and remained, unsigned, on his desk for another two days. A likely reason for his delay can be found in the account of Orville H. Browning, Illinois senator and Lincoln friend, who claimed the president told him he would not sign the bill into law until Governor Charles A. Wickliffe (at the time a congressman from Kentucky) could remove from the city "two family servants . . . who were sickly, and who would not be benefited by freedom."[42] In any case, when the president signed the bill on the sixteenth, he returned it to Congress with a note that expressed some concern. "I have never doubted the constitutional authority of Congress to abolish slavery in this district," he wrote, "and I have ever desired to see the national Capital freed from the institution in some satisfactory way."[43] He indicated objection to some aspect of the law but declined to specify that concern. Given his often-stated views on emancipation, it is likely that he disapproved of the people of the District not being given the opportunity to vote on the matter. What Lincoln also objected to, but was not willing to state in his message, was that the act rejected gradual emancipation, the president's preferred method to end slavery. According to Browning, Lincoln confided in him that "now families would at once be deprived of cooks, stable boys, &c and they [the enslaved laborers] of their protectors without any provision for them."[44] He was "gratified," however, that the act made provisions for compensation (to slaveholders, of course) and colonization, two features he felt essential to any program of emancipation.[45]

Energized by its success in implementing a plan for emancipation, Congress two months later outlawed slavery in the territories. Republican congressman Isaac Arnold of Illinois had introduced a bill in March 1862 that was designed to prohibit slavery in those areas where the federal government had jurisdiction. This included not only the territories but also various federal installations and the high seas. The comprehensive nature of the bill earned the disapproval of those who thought it challenged states' rights.[46] The final measure, "An Act to Secure Freedom to all Persons within the Territories of the United States," superseded the Supreme Court decision in *Dred Scott v. Sandford* in that it prohibited slavery or involuntary servitude in all existing territories as well as in those that might be acquired or formed in the future.[47] References to prohibition in federal installations and the high seas had been removed. As it matched his position on Congress's jurisdiction over the territories and secured the containment that he always believed was necessary to eventually eradicate slavery, Lincoln signed it without voicing objection or concern.

By the summer, Congress was prepared to venture beyond the territories to a more general emancipation. On July 17 it passed "an Act to suppress Insurrection, to punish Treason and Rebellion, to seize and confiscate the Property of Rebels." Essentially, the bill introduced by Senator Lyman Trumbull in December 1861 called for the seizure of property (human and otherwise) owned by anyone who was in rebellion against the government or who gave "aid and comfort" to such activity. The bill drew vociferous objection from both Democrats and Republicans, including Lincoln. In a message to Congress that accompanied the signed law, he delineated his concerns that it violated the constitutional guarantee that "no attainder of treason shall work corruption of blood, or forfeiture except during the life of the person attainted."[48] In other words, he considered it unconstitutional to deprive the heirs of the guilty party of the enjoyment of the property confiscated and freed. The unwieldy nature of the law (it required court action) and the Lincoln administration's lackluster attempts at enforcement left the measure unworkable.

That same day, Congress passed the Militia Act, which authorized the employment of people of African descent to labor in the construction of entrenchments and to work at tasks about camp "or any military or naval service for which they may be found competent." The law stipulated that any laborer so employed who had been owned by a disloyal individual would be freed, along with his wife, children, and mother.[49] Each man would receive ten dollars per month and rations, with three dollars reserved for clothing.

While Congress's efforts at emancipation generally met with presidential approval, the actions of certain generals continued to be problematic. In late April, Major General David Hunter, commander of Union forces in the Department of the South (which consisted of the states of South Carolina, Georgia, and Florida), declared martial law in the area under his command. Two weeks later, finding that "[s]lavery and martial law in a free country are altogether incompatible," Hunter declared all enslaved people in the three states "forever free." Unfortunately, the general had failed to inform the president of his actions; Lincoln heard of it through the newspapers. Denying that the government had received any official word of Hunter's declaration or that the administration had authorized it, he nullified Hunter's decree.

In objecting to Hunter's actions, Lincoln staked out a position that he was to draw on in the months to come. He suggested that *he* would decide the issue of emancipation if and when it became militarily necessary. He also took the opportunity to appeal to the border states once more, reminding them that they were in the best position to implement a program of gradual emancipation. "You cannot if you would, be blind to the signs of the times," he advised. "The change it contemplates would come gently as the dews of heaven, not rending or wrecking anything. Will you not embrace it?"[50]

The answer from the border states remained, emphatically, "No!," even after Lincoln appealed directly to their representatives. In a White House meeting on July 12, he warned them of the likelihood that their obstinacy would lead eventually to the loss of their enslaved laborers without compensation and that slavery would be "extinguished by mere friction and abrasion—by the mere incidents of the war." In an appeal to their patriotism, Lincoln assured them that they had the ability to hasten the end of the war.[51]

As he faced recalcitrant border states, abolitionist generals, and a proactive Congress, Lincoln also came under sustained pressure from proponents of freedom from the population at large. In June he met with a group of Progressive Quakers who represented the Chester County, Pennsylvania, community. The Friends denounced the actions of the Confederate states and labeled as "unchristian and barbarous" the institution at the center of their cause. They encouraged the president to seize the opportunity in his grasp to ensure the perpetuation of the Union and the preservation of its free institutions.[52]

Lincoln jokingly expressed his relief that they were not office seekers, since they were the most troublesome of the many things with which he had to contend. He then addressed the reason for their visit by attempting to convince them that a presidential decree would not have any effect in the South. He confessed a willingness to accept divine guidance on the matter of slavery but suggested that God might devise a plan that differed from what the Friends envisioned.[53]

In July the president met with another religious group, this time a committee representing the Synod of the Reformed Presbyterian Church, which presented him with resolutions the synod had recently passed on the matter of slavery. As with the Quakers, Lincoln empathized with the committee members in their desire to rid the country of slavery but indicated that thought had to be given to how best to accomplish it.[54] And when a group of Chicago Christians presented him with an emancipation memorial in September, just nine days before he issued the preliminary Emancipation Proclamation, he declined to share his pending action with them. Instead, he reiterated his often-declared sentiment that a proclamation issued by him would have little value. "Would *my word* free the slaves, when I cannot even enforce the Constitution in the rebel States?" he asked them. Lincoln proceeded to outline the challenges to issuing an emancipation decree, including the defection of the border states and the uncertainty of the value in arming black men. But contained within the response to the committee members was the acknowledgment that the president had the constitutional authority "as commander-in-chief of the army and navy, in time of war . . . to take any measure which may best subdue the enemy." He wished them to know as well that he had "not decided against a proclamation of liberty to the slaves" but held "the matter under advisement."[55]

Of course, Lincoln was being rather disingenuous. He had already decided to free those enslaved persons residing in the rebel states. The failure of the Peninsula Campaign (the result of General George B. McClellan's sluggish maneuvering), the lack of progress in getting the border states to implement plans of emancipation, the difficulty in securing volunteers, and the increasing pressure from abolition-inclined factions in the North—all had shaped his decision to act.

Taking advantage of the serenity of the Soldiers' Home, where he resided during the summer of 1862, Lincoln had found time to consider how he might justify issuing a presidential decree. Viewing emancipation from the precedents established by international laws of war, he concluded that his position as commander-in-chief gave him the authority, on the grounds of "military necessity," to quell the rebellion by seizing or destroying the property of the insurgents. But claims of "military necessity" could be tricky, especially with the world and opponents in the North scrutinizing his every move.[56] As he rode on July 13 with Secretaries William H. Seward and Gideon Welles to the funeral of the son of Secretary Edwin Stanton, Lincoln had revealed his intentions. The reaction of the two advisors—Wells remained speechless and Seward expressed concern about fallout not only from the South but among international elements as well—suggested that there would be no easy consensus.[57]

The response of the full cabinet a week later confirmed this. Secretary Stanton voiced his support of Lincoln's intention to pursue immediate military emancipation, while Montgomery Blair, fearful that such a proclamation would lead to the defection of the border states and disaster in the fall elections, objected strenuously. Gideon Welles and Caleb Smith chose to remain silent during the discussion and only later privately conveyed their concerns. Despite their commitment to abolition, Salmon Chase and William Seward cautioned Lincoln that such a bold measure might not be wise. Chase suggested a slower pace of emancipation, one shaped by the military's advance. Seward reiterated his concerns expressed in the July 13 carriage ride. His greatest fear was foreign intervention—that immediate emancipation would throw the South into chaos, disrupt the economy (especially the production of cotton on which the British and French were dependent), and force England and France to enter the war on the side of the Confederacy.

The concerns of his cabinet members did not deter Lincoln from his decision to proceed. He had only broached the subject to inform and entertain suggestions for improvement, not to seek their approval for action. However, he did accept Seward's suggestion that he wait for a Union battlefield victory before releasing the proclamation so as not to look like the action was "the last measure of an exhausted government, a cry for help . . . our last shriek, on the retreat."[58] It would be two long months before the opportunity arose to issue the preliminary Emancipation Proclamation.

In the meantime, the president sought to lay a foundation for least resistance to emancipation. Believing that white Americans would find it difficult if not impossible to tolerate large numbers of free black people in their midst, he proposed voluntary colonization of anyone freed during the war and others within the African American population who might be inclined to go. Colonization was not a novel idea for black men and women. In the first quarter of the century, black emigrationists, for reasons shaped by a combination of misguided altruism toward the indigenous population and concern for the well-being of fellow African Americans, had sought to establish settlements outside of the United States. A black Massachusetts ship captain, Paul Cuffe, had encouraged emigration to help "civilize" and "Christianize" Africa. In 1815 he transported a group of thirty-eight settlers to Sierra Leone at his own expense. A decade later, in 1824, Richard Allen and James Forten founded the Haytian Emigration Society of Coloured People, an organization that eventually facilitated the resettlement of several hundred African Americans to both Haiti and the Dominican Republic. During the antebellum period and early in the war, others such as James T. Holley, Henry Highland Garnet (founder of the African Civilization Society), and Martin Delany, believing that a better life awaited African Americans in a foreign land, had championed immigration to either the Caribbean islands or to the African continent.[59] One of the most prominent black men in Washington, Henry McNeal Turner, pastor of the Israel Bethel African Methodist Episcopal Church, encouraged debate on the issue of colonization. In June 1862, approximately 150 black men and women, many of them residents of Washington, had left America for an uncertain future in Haiti.[60]

Despite the lack of uniformity in the opinions of black men and women themselves over the issue of colonization, Lincoln's position on the subject had riled many in the African American community. When in December 1861 the president proposed that Congress appropriate funds for resettlement of those persons seized through the First Confiscation Act or freed through state action, the editor of the *Weekly Anglo-African* suggested, sarcastically, "any surplus change Congress may have can be appropriated with our consent to expatriate and settle elsewhere the surviving slaveholders."[61] John Rock, freeborn abolitionist, doctor, and lawyer, asked, "Why is it that the people from all other countries are invited to come here, and we are asked to go away? . . . Does anyone pretend to deny that this is our country? or that much of the wealth and prosperity found here is the result of the labor of our hands? or that our blood and bones have not crimsoned and whitened every battle-field from Maine to Louisiana?"[62] Sentiment against emigration was so emotion-charged by the summer of 1862 that agents and colonization promoters were sometimes physically attacked.[63]

The president's mid-August meeting with a delegation of black men from the African American community elicited a similar response. James Mitchell, "Commissioner of Emigration" (and a man not altogether trusted by African Americans), facilitated the invitation to the White House. Mitchell had contacted the black churches and conveyed Lincoln's interest in talking with a representative group about colonization. The five men selected were all prominent members of the African American community—Edward Thomas, leader of the group and active in various fraternal orders and in fund-raising for the National Freedmen's Relief Association; John F. Cook Jr., like his father, an educator; Benjamin McCoy, founder of Asbury Methodist Church; Cornelius Clark, a member of the Social Civil and Statistical Association (an organization whose membership consisted of some of the most elite black men in the city); and John Costin, whose family had been a prominent fixture in the African American community for decades.[64]

Lincoln did not seek the opinions of the black men present but instead lectured them on the advantages of colonization—to black people as well as to the nation. Whether the incident had been intended to make emancipation more palatable to white men and women by assuring them that they need not feel threatened by a black presence or whether it reflected the president's assessment of race relations in

America and his own attitudes about the African American capacity to fit into American society as a free people, African Americans did not appreciate the president's candor.

Lincoln began by suggesting that there was perhaps a greater difference between the black and white races than between any other two groups among humankind and that this difference made it virtually impossible for the two races to coexist. The war, he continued, resulted from the presence of black people and the institution that kept them in bondage. To this extent, both groups suffered. Lincoln acknowledged that black men and women were forced to endure "the greatest wrong inflicted on any people," but he did not envision a change once slavery was eradicated. The current condition of freed people suggested that even in freedom, African American men and women could not expect equality at home. "[N]ot a single man of your race is made the equal of a single man of ours," he argued. "Go where you are treated the best, and the ban is still upon you." Separation, then, was the logical solution. Colonization, perhaps in Central America, under the leadership of "intelligent colored men" such as those present, could save the black population from further suffering and would allow them to control their future.[65]

Black people bristled at the suggestion that they were the cause of the war and that it would be in their best interest if they voluntarily left the country. Frederick Douglass characteristically blasted Lincoln for his unworkable plan to solve the racial problem in America. "The President of the United States seems to possess an ever increasing passion for making himself appear silly and ridiculous," he wrote. "Mr. Lincoln assumes the language and arguments of an itinerant Colonization lecturer, showing all his inconsistencies, his pride of race and blood, his contempt for negroes and his canting hypocrisy."[66] Thirty-year-old Alfred P. Smith, journalist and editor from Saddle River, New Jersey, reminded the president that black people were patriotic Americans who loved their country as much as he did. In a response to the president's suggestion that those colonized could perhaps mine coal in Central America, Smith invited him to "give McClellan some, give Halleck some, and by all means, save a little strip for yourself."[67] Frances Ellen Watkins Harper, famed poet and abolitionist, joined the chorus of disapproval. "If Jeff Davis does not colonize Lincoln out of Washington, let him be thankful," she offered. "The president's dabbling with colonization just now suggests to my mind the idea of a man dying with a loathsome cancer, and busying himself with having his hair trimmed according to the latest fashion."[68] George B. Vashon, attorney, essayist, and future president of Avery College, had lived in Haiti for almost three years. He did not explicitly object to emigration, but he feared that Lincoln's comments would encourage white men in their assertion that African Americans had no claim to the land of their birth. Such a thing as removal, even voluntarily, was unjust. In an open letter to Lincoln, Vashon declared, "The white man's oppression of the negro, and not the negro himself, has brought upon the nation the leprosy under which it groans. The negro may be the scab indicative of the disease, but his removal . . . will not effect a cure."[69]

Two weeks after meeting with the black delegation, the president continued to employ the ruse that he had not made any decisions on slavery. Horace Greeley, editor of the *New York Tribune*, who penned a cutting editorial titled "The Prayer of Twenty Millions," presented the opportunity to him. Greeley had criticized Lincoln for his alleged failure to execute the laws, especially as they applied to the Second Confiscation Act; for failing to reproach his generals who were ignoring the emancipating provisions of the act; for bending to the interests of the border state representatives; and for treating traitors with deference. Greeley reminded Lincoln of an incident in which a group of black men, enslaved by sugar planters thirty miles outside of New Orleans, had made their way to the Union-occupied city. Instead of securing their freedom, as Greeley believed the Second Confiscation Act had intended, the men were attacked and either reenslaved or killed. The excuse, apparently, was that they were armed, but evidence suggested that they were simply in possession of "their implements of daily labor in the cane-field." Greeley argued that the loyal millions cried out for the president to "render a hearty and unequivocal obedience to the law of the land."[70]

Lincoln's response to Greeley's admonishment came three days later in a letter addressed to the editor. "If there be those who would not save the Union unless they could at the same time *destroy* slavery, I do not agree with them," he wrote. "My paramount object in this struggle *is* to save the Union, and is *not* either to save or destroy slavery." Lincoln explained that he would do whatever preserved the Union, be it freeing all, some, or none of the enslaved people. "What I do about slavery, and the colored race," he argued, "I do because I believe it helps to save the Union; and what I forbear, I forbear because I do *not* believe it helps to save the Union." The president hastened to say that this was his "view of official duty," but that he still maintained the personal desire that "all men everywhere could be free."[71]

When just over a week before issuing the preliminary Emancipation Proclamation, Lincoln received an emancipation memorial signed by Chicago ministers of various Christian denominations, he was still shielding his intentions while subtly preparing the public for what was about to occur. He assured the ministers who delivered the memorial that slavery and emancipation had occupied his thoughts for some time. Although he desired to know and do the will of God, he did not expect any revelation, as this was not "the days of miracles." Instead, he would have to study the matter and glean an answer. In the meantime, a proclamation of emancipation would be of no more use than the "Pope's bull against the comet!" Then, in language that foreshadowed the proclamation he would issue on September 22, Lincoln suggested that he had no legal or constitutional objections against an emancipating decree, "for as commander-in-chief of the army and navy, in time of war, I suppose I have a right to take any measure which may best subdue the enemy." Neither did he have objections on moral grounds, as others had who feared that an unchained black population would rise up and commit all sorts of atrocities against their former masters. Lincoln viewed emancipation as "a practical war measure, to be decided upon according to the advantages or disadvantages it may offer" to ending the war.[72] It was a point he would repeat many times as he took charge of the emancipation process in the fall of 1862.

Abraham Lincoln on battlefield at Antietam, Maryland. This photograph, taken by Alexander Gardner on October 3, 1862, shows Abraham Lincoln with General George B. McClellan after a Union victory on September 17 gave the president the opportunity to issue a proclamation of freedom. Lincoln had been counseled to wait for a battlefield victory before issuing a proclamation so that it would not be misconstrued as an act of desperation. Library of Congress, Prints and Photographs Division; reproduction number LC-USZ62–2276.

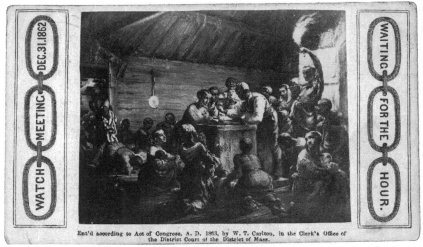

"Watch meeting, Dec. 31, 1862—Waiting for the Hour," 1863. In the hours before President Lincoln issued the Emancipation Proclamation, African Americans gathered in public places and in private homes in anticipation of good news. Watch night services became a tradition that lasted for many years in certain areas of the country. Library of Congress, Prints and Photographs Division; reproduction number LC-DIG-ppms-ca-10981USZ62–123456.

"Emancipation," 1865. The Thomas Nast image of emancipation illustrates the promise of the Emancipation Proclamation. Depicted are joyous domestic scenes and those of unexploited and uncoerced labor juxtaposed with the general degradation and oppression of slavery. Library of Congress, Prints and Photographs Division; reproduction number LC-DIG-pga-03898.

U.S. Colored Troops, Company E, Fourth U.S. Colored Infantry, Fort
Lincoln (District of Columbia). In May 1863 Congress formed the Bureau
of Colored Troops after President Lincoln authorized the enlistment of
African American men into the regular army under the provisions of the
Emancipation Proclamation. Eventually nearly two hundred thousand
black soldiers and sailors would serve in defense of the Union and free-
dom. Photograph by William Morris Smith, circa 1863–65. Library of
Congress, Prints and Photographs Division; reproduction number LC-
DIG-cwpb-04294.

EMANCIPATION BY
PRESIDENTIAL DECREE

As one organization or critic after another questioned his commitment to liberty or gently pressed him to move forward with
an emancipating edict, Lincoln remained resolute that he would not
move too soon. When he disclosed his plans to the cabinet in July, he
agreed to wait for a Union victory. Doubtless, he did not imagine that
the opportunity to declare freedom would be weeks away. When the
Army of the Potomac engaged the Army of Northern Virginia near
the town of Sharpsburg in Maryland on the morning of September
17, Union fortunes on the battlefield shifted, and along with it came
a change in fortune for African Americans.

The Battle of Antietam was hardly the victory for which Lincoln or
the Union had hoped. Although George B. McClellan forced Robert
E. Lee to retreat, the battle itself, including the events of September 17
(infamously designated the single bloodiest day in American military
history), was a draw. Nevertheless, it gave Lincoln the opportunity
he needed to expand the aim of the war. Hence, on September 22,
1862, he issued an ultimatum to the Confederate states: return to the
Union by January 1 or the enslaved population would be freed. For
the next hundred days, opponents and proponents of freedom alike
anxiously waited to see if the president would execute his threat.

The preliminary Emancipation Proclamation was a curious mix-
ture of warning and reassurance. Lincoln restated the aim of the
war, "practically restoring the constitutional relation" between the

seceded states and the Union. He also indicated that he would again propose to Congress that it financially assist any slaveholding Union states that desired to institute either immediate or gradual abolition. The freed people would be colonized, with their consent. Those states or parts of states that remained in rebellion on January 1, however, would suffer the loss of their enslaved property. Anyone who had remained loyal to the Union would be compensated for their loss.[1]

The reaction in the Confederate South was swift and emphatic. One week after Lincoln issued the preliminary decree, the Confederate Congress responded by passing a joint resolution introduced by Senator Thomas J. Semmes of Louisiana asserting that "the Proclamation of Abraham Lincoln . . . is leveled against the citizens of the confederate States and as such is a gross violation of the usages of civilized warfare, an outrage on their rights of private property, and an invitation to an atrocious servile war, and therefore should be held up to the execration of mankind, and counteracted by such severe retaliatory measures as in the judgment of the President may be calculated to secure its withdrawal or arrest its execution."[2] A call came to make it a capital offense for any commissioned or non-commissioned officer to incite rebellion among the enslaved or to promise freedom under the provisions of the proclamation. Others suggested an abandonment of civilized warfare and the adoption of a war of extermination.

The abolitionist press made much of rumors that the Confederacy was in utter terror at the prospect of the proclamation's taking effect. The rebels "express fears that it will be the means of producing a counter revolution in the slave States," reported a correspondent of the *New York Times*, "and the soldiers desire to return to their homes to protect their families. They believe the negroes are organized in scores, and only waiting an opportunity to rise in insurrection. They have heard already of the Proclamation, and are becoming very restive under the yoke. . . . A private circular has been issued by the rebel government to the proprietors of newspapers, forbidding the publication of the Proclamation."[3]

That the Confederacy feared the proclamation, even before it went into effect, can perhaps be gleaned from an alleged incident in

Culpeper County, Virginia, in October. Fear of retaliation from a long-aggrieved people led local residents to arrest a dozen or more free and enslaved black men, whom they charged with conspiracy and, according to contemporary accounts, eventually hanged. Their crime, apparently, was being in possession of a copy of Lincoln's decree. "The fact that such a proclamation has been made is well known among all the negroes," the *National Republican* reported. "And it produces the most startling effect. The terror of the whites is beyond description. . . . Apprehensions of re-enactment of the Nat Turner horrors are felt to an alarming degree."[4]

The northern response to the preliminary proclamation was, in general, quite positive. "There can be no state paper imagined more noble than one which carries substantial liberty to millions of slaves," reported the *New York Independent*. "The Proclamation is the drawing of a sword that can never be sheathed again. . . . Let sorrows fall fast; there is joy before us!" The *Hartford Courant* agreed. "We rejoice most heartily that the axe is laid to the root of the tree," it exclaimed. "The Proclamation meets our views both in what it does, and in what it omits to do. Its limitations show that President Lincoln means to preserve good faith toward the loyal border slave States. So long as they are loyal, their slaves are safe." Many believed that any effort taken to end the war, even freeing the enslaved population, was acceptable.[5] The president had acted in moderation and had given due notice of his intentions. The preliminary proclamation also won the support of the Union governors who attended a conference in Altoona, Pennsylvania, just two days after Lincoln made his announcement. His decision to emancipate halted the criticism of several of those in attendance who had pressed him to quell the southern rebellion by seizing the enslaved laborers.

The black community, both in the North and in the South, enslaved and free, greeted the news of promised emancipation with surprise, ebullience, and a bit of apprehension. The excitement that permeated the African American community virtually exploded from the pages of the *Christian Recorder*. Its editor wrote, "The world moves. We are living years in days, and centuries in years." Understanding that Lincoln's action was the result of military necessity, the newspaper saw it nonetheless as carrying "a moral power which is irresistible. It draws the lines between liberty and slavery, and boldly sets the Government before the world on the side of liberty for all men."[6]

A gigantic step had been taken, but freedom was not assured. African Americans and the allies of freedom found themselves in the awkward position of praying for Union victories on the battlefield but hoping for a less-than-sweeping defeat of Confederate forces. The freedom promised in the preliminary proclamation depended upon the Confederacy's failure to dissolve itself and return to the Union by January 1. Few Americans gave serious credence to the idea that peace would or *could* be restored before the proclamation took effect. Indeed, the prevailing wisdom held that the Confederates had no reason to acquiesce. Their own successes on the battlefield and Union bungling had only strengthened their belief that ultimate victory would be theirs. General McClellan's continued reluctance to advance his Army of the Potomac had sustained Confederate dominance in the East and earned the acerbic criticism of those eager to see serious movement against the rebels. Lincoln's eventual replacement of McClellan with General Ambrose E. Burnside in early November did little to strengthen the Union position in the field. The army's abysmal showing at Fredericksburg in mid-December demoralized the Union forces and left northerners questioning the Lincoln administration's ability to wage an effective war.[7]

While the Confederacy seemed to be able to withstand whatever military might the Union possessed, and hence to meet the stipulation for being in rebellion on January 1, there remained myriad pressures that could have convinced Lincoln to rescind the proclamation. Foremost among them was opposition emanating from various northern groups that remained proslavery and who had insisted on reunification with the institution intact. While abolitionists and Radical Republicans generally supported the president's pronouncement, the more conservative members of Lincoln's own party, northern Democrats, and political leaders in the border states condemned it. Conservatives argued that Lincoln lacked the constitutional authority to declare enslaved property free. "The whole world will laugh at the impotence of this mere Paper Thunder," the *New York Express* predicted. "The President . . . is, in the utterance of this Proclamation, doing his best to divide the Northern States, and to split them up into parties, as well as . . . prolonging the war indefinitely." The *Boston Courier* argued that the decree was little more than Lincoln's attempt to placate the radicals and that it would "have no more effect upon the slaves in the Southern States, than if Mr. Lincoln should order the north wind to blow continuously over the Southern fields, in order to produce a change in the atmosphere."[8] Others concluded that the proclamation would derail the efforts of Unionists in the border states and would lead to their defection, something Lincoln himself had assiduously attempted to avoid in executing his wartime policies. Indeed, border state Unionists who were slaveholders viewed the president's action as a betrayal of their rights and an affront to their loyalty to the administration. Still other opponents charged that Lincoln's actions would prolong the war by giving the secessionists greater reason to fight. Southern men would rally to the Confederate cause rather than allow black men, freed by Lincoln's proclamation, to rise up in revolt.[9] "We can see nothing but evil and trouble and disasters to come from this last step of President Lincoln," the *Weekly Vincennes Western Sun* declared. "God save our poor, bleeding country!" The *Louisville Journal* called it "a wholly unauthorized and wholly pernicious" measure. "Kentucky cannot and will not acquiesce in this measure. Never!"[10]

Proponents of freedom also worried that certain military men— officers and the rank and file alike—would make good on their threat that any attempt to expand the goal of the war to one that included freedom for the enslaved would be met with wholesale desertion. Northern soldiers held no fonder opinions of enslaved people than did the civilian population they had left behind. Men willing to risk all for union had little if any interest in laying down their lives for persons they thought to be inferior and who they believed were likely to be in competition with them for jobs after the war had ended.

The threat of Democratic ascendancy in the fall elections gave Republicans and abolitionists particular cause for concern. Northern Democrats quickly seized on dissatisfaction with the proclamation to increase their ranks in Congress. In the Midwest (specifically Ohio, Indiana, and Illinois), Democratic candidates garnered support from voters by convincing them that African Americans freed by the proclamation would flood their states in search of employment. In fact, a series of race riots had broken out in the Midwest during the summer of 1862, whose impetus was fear of economic competition. Elsewhere, concerns over Lincoln's suspension of the writ of habeas corpus and disappointment with meager Union victories combined with opposition to emancipation to make Republican defeat likely.

Of particular interest to most Republicans was the gubernatorial race in the state of New York, where General James S. Wadsworth, an abolitionist, opposed Democratic candidate Horatio Seymour. Seymour and the Democratic Party had appealed to voters by embracing a platform that called the Emancipation Proclamation "a proposal for the butchery of women and children, for scenes of lust and rapine, and of arson and murder." Loyal Unionists believed that Seymour had ventured dangerously out of bounds by declaring that if the Union could be saved only through emancipation, "then the people of the South should be allowed to withdraw themselves from the government" because it gave them no protection of their rights.[11]

Interest in the Seymour-Wadsworth campaign underscored the significance of New York to both the Union cause and the success of the proclamation. As the most populous state in the Union, New York would serve as the measure of Republican strength in general and of support for Lincoln's administration in particular. "If [the Democratic] party can be overwhelmingly defeated in this State . . . the President's Emancipation policy will be put into full execution on the first day of January, and the country will enter upon the only road to permanent security and peace," Frederick Douglass believed. "It is clear that he who at this crisis votes for Horatio Seymour, votes against the loyal administration, and in effect for Jefferson Davis and his rebel Government."[12]

With the elections over, the Republicans assessed the damage they had suffered. The Democrats enjoyed an increase of thirty-four seats in Congress, with five states—Illinois, Indiana, New York, Ohio, and Pennsylvania—returning majority Democratic delegations. The

Democrats experienced gains in several state legislatures as well. And in New York, Seymour dashed the hopes of the Republicans. These Democratic successes, however, were not stunning defeats, as some historians have claimed. In reality, the Republicans retained a twenty-five-seat majority in the House of Representatives, increased the number of Senate seats they occupied by five, and controlled seventeen of nineteen governorships and sixteen of the state legislatures. Even when the Democrats won, the margin of victory was small.[13]

If a divided North threatened to undermine emancipation, there was no less concern about the role Great Britain might play in the unfolding drama. From the very beginning of the war, northerners had been concerned with keeping England from recognizing Confederate independence. Such action would have legitimized the rebellion and perhaps would have led to military support. Driving a wedge between the Confederate states and their European economic partners was one of the primary motivations for Lincoln's issuing the proclamation. He hoped that once the Union committed itself to liberation of the enslaved, the British—who had already embraced free labor—would be unable to support the slaveholding Confederacy.

The British middle and working classes supported abolitionism, but their government had the more practical task of ensuring the economic health of the nation. The government's initial reaction to the preliminary proclamation had not encouraged the Lincoln administration. In the October 8 *London Post*, British prime minister Lord Palmerston had judged the proclamation "a singular manifesto that could scarcely be treated seriously. . . . How utterly powerless and contemptible a government must have become which could sanction with its approval such . . . trash."[14] The British press was hardly less indicting of Lincoln's action. They either condemned the proclamation as meaningless or charged that it would incite the enslaved to revolt. The paper most influential with the average reader, the London *Times*, was especially vociferous in its condemnation, and blatantly racist as well. The *Times* accused Lincoln of "appeal[ing] to the black blood of the African; he will whisper of the pleasures of spoil and of the gratification of yet fiercer instincts; and when blood begins to flow and shrieks come piercing through the darkness, Mr. Lincoln will wait till the rising flames tell that all is consummated, and then he will rub his hands and think that revenge is sweet."[15]

Given the many factors that could derail final implementation of the proclamation, supporters of emancipation criticized Lincoln's decision to issue a warning rather than to declare freedom immediately. Even Frederick Douglass, who had such strong words of praise when Lincoln had originally announced his intentions, now reassessed the document with more sober reflection. In Douglass's estimation, Lincoln had progressed toward emancipation "like an ox under the yoke, or a Slave under the lash." In reevaluating the proclamation, he found it absent any humanitarian impulse: "His words kindled no enthusiasm. They touched neither justice nor mercy. He moved, but was moved by necessity.—Emancipation—is put off—it was made future and conditional—not present and absolute."[16]

Abolitionists found reason for worry in Lincoln's annual message to Congress in December. Instead of mentioning the Emancipation Proclamation that was scheduled for implementation in just a few weeks, the president outlined a proposed constitutional amendment that would provide for compensation for any state seeking to end slavery before century's end! Although this gradual plan of emancipation would permit bondage to continue for another thirty-seven years, Lincoln justified it as ultimately eliminating the institution throughout the land because it would exceed the provisions of the preliminary Emancipation Proclamation. And returning to his belief in gradualism, he argued that a slower process rather than immediate emancipation would "spare both races from the evils of sudden derangement" and would ensure that those who had objected most to freeing the enslaved would have "passed away before its consummation."[17] To this he added his continuing support for the colonization of those African Americans thus freed.

Despite Lincoln's seeming disregard for his own ultimatum, he declared freedom at the appointed time. In the early afternoon of January 1, he signed the fateful document after, legend has it, pausing momentarily to steady his trembling hand. The seeming hesitation was brought on, supposedly, not by the momentous occasion but rather by three hours of greeting guests who had come to the White

House to wish him well. Given the enormity of his actions, one would not have been surprised had the unsteadiness been caused by a moment of doubt.

By design, Lincoln's proclamation was an ineloquent, legal document, almost totally devoid of any outwardly humanitarian sentiment. Concerned about judicial challenge, the president drew on his constitutional authority as commander-in-chief to seize the property of the enemy to end a revolt. While the popular perception has been that he "freed the slaves with a stroke of his pen," the proclamation, like most things, was far more complex. The final document, issued as "a fit and necessary war measure," declared approximately 3.1 million enslaved people free in the seceded states. Roughly 830,000 African Americans remained untouched by the document's provisions, including those in the border states—Missouri, Kentucky, Maryland, and Delaware—certain areas of Virginia and Louisiana (where the Union military already prevailed, hence not meeting the stipulations of "necessary war measure"), and Tennessee, where a Unionist government under the leadership of Andrew Johnson had been established. Lincoln pledged that the federal authorities (including the military) would maintain the freedom of those liberated and directed African Americans to remain peaceful, "unless in necessary self-defense," and to work for "reasonable wages."[18]

Lincoln had always paired black freedom with colonization and compensation to owners for the loss of their property, but no such stipulations appeared in the final proclamation. Instead, the needs of the Union military overrode the desire for colonization and protection of property rights. Henceforward, black men would be allowed to don the Union blue. The president authorized that they be permitted to "garrison forts, positions, stations, and other places, and to man vessels of all sorts." In essence, they would be allowed to fight for preservation of the Union as well as for the maintenance of their own freedom and for the liberation of their brothers and sisters.

The president ended the proclamation with a reiteration of the constitutional grounds for its being issued—that of military necessity. But he also declared it "an act of justice" and appealed to "the considerate judgment of mankind, and the gracious favor of

Almighty God." The addition was suggested by Secretary of the Treasury Salmon P. Chase, who believed that "on an occasion of such interest, there can be no just imputation of affection against a solemn recognition of responsibility before men and before God."[19] The final words imbued the document with some degree of moral sentiment and rescued it from the legalistic tone Lincoln had deliberately employed throughout.

The final proclamation encouraged responses as varied as those accompanying the preliminary document. On December 31 and January 1, freedom's supporters had gathered in cities throughout the North to await word that the president had fulfilled his promise. In Boston, three thousand converged on Tremont Temple, where they passed the time listening to some of the best-known abolitionists of the day: Frederick Douglass, Anna E. Dickinson, J. Sella Martin, and William Wells Brown. The news finally reached them late in the evening on January 1, launching a celebration that did not end, even after they were shut out of Tremont Temple at midnight. The exuberant gathering then retired to Twelfth Street Baptist Church and did not disband until daybreak.[20] Shiloh Presbyterian Church was the site of apprehension and ultimate elation in New York. There, on New Year's Eve, the Reverend Henry Highland Garnet presided over a gathering that overflowed with an audience, nearly one-third of which was white.[21] And in the nation's capital, Reverend Henry McNeal Turner, a bishop in the African Methodist Episcopal Church, joined others assembled at Israel Bethel AME in thanksgiving for the day of deliverance. Years later, Turner would recall that upon hearing that Lincoln had issued the proclamation, "men squealed, women fainted . . . white and colored people shook hands, songs were sung. . . . Every face had a smile and even the dumb animals seemed to realize that some extraordinary event had taken place."[22]

Watch night vigils gave way to "grand jubilees" once the proclamation had been issued. An "intelligent, respectable, joyous," and orderly audience overflowed Cooper Union in New York on January 5, where celebrants listened to prominent abolitionist Lewis Tappan and others. At Plymouth Church in Brooklyn, the Reverend Henry Ward Beecher placed the Emancipation Proclamation in the context of the struggle between good and evil. Taking as his text Revelation 18:1–8, he saw the war as "two opposing forces for the government of the continent—the spirit of Christian liberty and democracy, and the spirit of aristocratic oppression." Beecher recognized that the proclamation "may not immediately free a single slave," but he believed that it imbued liberty with a "moral recognition."[23]

Frederick Douglass was similarly encouraged. Shortly after the decree was issued, an exuberant Douglass suggested that the proclamation was "the greatest event of our nation's history if not the greatest event of the century."[24] Although it excluded enslaved people from the border states, the existence of contiguous free states would ultimately destroy slavery everywhere. Douglass saw the proclamation as a revolutionary document. Not only did it destroy the legal status of human property and admit blacks into the American family, but in facilitating the ending of slavery, the decree also liberated white men by freeing them from the contradictions in their own government. Furthermore, it joined the nation and the American people to the larger struggle for human liberty throughout the world. While Lincoln had emphasized military necessity as justification for emancipation, Douglass chose to see the proclamation as a "grand *moral* necessity."[25]

Of course, not all abolitionists agreed. A contributor to William Lloyd Garrison's *Liberator* accused Lincoln of possessing neither "high principle" nor "eminent wisdom" and admonished him for letting the opportunity to end slavery everywhere slip from his grasp. In his estimation, Lincoln had deliberately preferred to "'scotch' the snake, instead of killing it."[26]

Northern conservatives and many Democrats continued their criticism of emancipation as well. The *New York Herald* saw the final decree as "practically a dead letter" that "amounts to nothing as a measure of emancipation. The advocates of 'human rights' upon the basis of negro equality will be sorely puzzled to comprehend the humanity, justice or consistency of these remarkable discriminations of Mr. Lincoln in favor of slavery where he may practically proclaim freedom, and in favor of liberty where he has no power to enforce it; but it must be remembered that this edict is a war measure, and that negro philanthropy has nothing to do with it." The newspaper considered the proclamation unconstitutional and unnecessary and likely to be the downfall of the Lincoln administration. The result would be to unite white men throughout the South and ensure Union defeat. The *Herald* encouraged the Lincoln administration to prosecute the war, "not for negro emancipation, but for the restoration of the Union and the constitution in their integrity."[27]

Fear spread among conservatives that such radical action would destroy any chances that a compromise could be reached and the war brought to a speedier conclusion. "If we gently whisper 'PEACE!,'" one contemporary suggested, "we are forthwith adjudged a traitor, and followed by the howls of the Abolition horde."[28] Even residents of Lincoln's home state passed resolutions condemning his actions. Notable among them was the resolution passed by a large gathering of antiwar Democrats and opponents of the proclamation who had met in the Hall of Representatives of the General Assembly on the evening of January 5. The attendees (which included not only certain Democratic members of the legislature but other residents from across the state) declared the proclamation "as unwarrantable in military as in civil law; a gigantic usurpation, at once converting the war, professedly commenced by the administration for the vindication of the authority of the constitution, into a crusade for the sudden, unconditional and violent liberation of three millions of negro slaves." They feared a race war that would lead to unspeakable crimes on both sides "and which the civilized world will denounce, as an ineffaceable disgrace to the American name."[29]

As Lincoln had feared, some of the greatest opposition to the proclamation came from the border states, whose stubborn resistance to state-mandated emancipation had frustrated his efforts and ultimately convinced him to act on his own. Their supposed loyalty to the Union was secondary, at best, to their self-interest in maintaining the institution of slavery. Representative of their response is an editorial from the *Louisville Democrat*, which declared with no small degree of irony: "We scarcely know how to express our indignation at this flagrant outrage of all Constitutional law, all human justice, all Christian feeling. . . . To think that we, who have been the foremost in the grand march of civilization, should be so disgraced by an imbecile President as to be made to appear before the world as the encourager of insurrection, lust, arson, and murder."[30]

Nowhere was the final proclamation more reviled than in the Confederate South, where it was greeted with disdain and bravado. White secessionists considered Lincoln's decree an abomination and tried to dismiss it as meaningless. In the capital of the Confederacy, the *Daily Dispatch* predicted that "no proclamation which the Yankees have issued, or may issue, will have the *slightest* effect upon the slave population of the South. . . . 'Cursed be Canaan; a servant of servants shall he be to his brethren,' is a proclamation which even the mighty Abraham Lincoln cannot abolish."[31]

But Confederate president Jefferson Davis knew better. He considered the decree an attempt to provoke "the most execrable massacre recorded in the history of guilty man." Predicting that the proclamation would inspire a bloody revolt, he assailed Lincoln for placing the good white people of the South in danger of a servile insurrection and for inviting the extermination of "millions of human beings of an inferior race, peaceful and contented laborers," the ultimate result of such an insurrection.[32]

In the coming weeks and months, the Confederate South would feel even more strongly the strain imposed by black freedom, as the proclamation's impact bore fruit. Notwithstanding the bravado of the *Daily Dispatch*, the southern states would witness an extraordinary transformation that would upend the social relationships in the region and alter the economic system. The formerly enslaved would seize upon the opportunities introduced by the proclamation and make it their own.

TO KNOW FREEDOM

A *New York Tribune* correspondent traveling through the Confederate South in the early spring of 1863 observed the sentiment of freedmen and freedwomen toward their former owners. "It is singular how totally devoid the Negroes of Mississippi, Louisiana, and every other Cotton State in which I have been during the progress of the war, are of fealty to their masters," he reported. Contradicting the boast by southern planters that their "people" would never abandon them, the correspondent found that the enslaved "seem to have a passionate love for liberty, and are constantly incurring risks in its behalf. . . . Not only field hands, but house servants . . . with a strange ingratitude run away at the first opportunity, weaning themselves at once and for ever from the charms of slavery." On one plantation, the property of ex-senator William Gwin of California (a Democrat and southern sympathizer), he found the slave quarters deserted by laborers "oblivious of the debt of affection they owed" to their owners.[1]

This observation could have been made from any part of the Confederacy—the Upper South as well as those states that made up the cotton kingdom. Throughout the region, black men and women tested the Emancipation Proclamation's force by discarding traditional modes of behavior and relationships. Some fled the plantations, while others either never got the change to do so or were convinced by their own circumstances to remain in place. Whether staying or fleeing, they facilitated Union victory and helped to secure their own freedom by destroying slavery.

News of the proclamation did not reach every enslaved person immediately or in the same way. Many found out roughly at the same time as their owners, long before Union troops arrived to liberate them. Others got the first word through rumors passed along by the astonishingly efficient slave "grapevine telegraph," seemingly the best alternative for a people denied literacy. Susie Melton of Virginia learned she was free when "a Yankee soldier tole someone in Williamsburg" that Lincoln had signed the proclamation. Despite the bitter cold, enslaved people on Melton's plantation celebrated through the night, and in the morning they walked away, eager to embrace a life of freedom. "Didn't care nothin' bout Missus," she recalled. "[W]as goin' to Union lines."[2]

Benjamin Holmes learned of the proclamation while he was being held in a South Carolina slave pen, where he had been placed after his owner sold him to a trader. Holmes had learned to read, and he was able to share with other inmates of the pen the news he found in a discarded paper. "Such rejoicing as there was then!" he later recalled. "One old man held a prayer meeting right there in the mart." Despite the good news, however, Holmes did not secure his freedom until a year later, after he had been transported to Tennessee. Thomas Rutling, a native Tennessean, received word of the proclamation from his owner's son, a young doctor who apparently abhorred slavery and had spread the news of emancipation throughout the quarters. To Rutling's child's mind (he was about nine years old in 1863), freedom would bring all that white men possessed. He would remember later that he "decide[d] in a moment what kind of a horse" he would acquire.[3]

Technically, the proclamation's provisions did not free Rutling and Holmes, residents of an exempted state, but their liberation underscores the impact that the decree had even on those who were not meant to benefit from it. Provisions for the recruitment of black men into the military with the consent of loyal owners facilitated freedom in Tennessee and the border states. Even when the owners did not give consent, it was difficult to prevent recruiting agents from impressing or persuading black men to come into the Union ranks.[4]

Those who lived in remote areas sometimes did not learn that they were free until well after the proclamation was issued or even after the war had ended. Henri Necaise of Pearl River County, Mississippi, recalled that he did not find out that he was free until his owner attempted to beat him. At that point, the owner's son intervened and reminded his father that the proclamation had set Necaise free.[5] Others, such as Louis Hughes, had to run away after the war had ended. "We knew it was our right to be free, for the proclamation had long been issued," Hughes recalled in his autobiography. "Yet they still held us." The thirty-one-year-old had fled his plantation in Mississippi on June 26, 1865, with another illegally enslaved man. Expecting retaliation from their owners when they returned to retrieve their families, the men enlisted the aid of two soldiers from Union headquarters in Memphis. With the assistance of these men, the group finally reached freedom on July 4.[6] And in Galveston, Texas, the enslaved population did not receive official word of emancipation until June 19, 1865, when Major General Gordon Granger read General Orders No. 3, informing the residents that "in accordance with a proclamation from the Executive of the United States, all slaves are free." The order reminded white men and women that there was now "an absolute equality of personal rights and rights of property" between former owners and freed people. But Union soldiers continued to treat the freedmen and freedwomen as though they were property by requiring them to list the names of their former owners and directing them to seek employment where they currently resided.[7]

It did not take long, however, for many to discover that the proclamation existed, and they resolved to wait no longer than was necessary to seize their freedom. Just two days after the decree took effect, the *Christian Recorder* reported that "the Negroes [of Mississippi] are in great numbers coming into Gen. Grant's line, bringing horses, mules, and wagons." Within one month, the state's black laborers were "flying away in every direction."[8]

In issuing the proclamation, Lincoln knew that it would be effective only if it encouraged black men and women to "come bodily over from the rebel side to ours."[9] Although it is difficult to determine how many were actually induced to flee, it can be surmised that flight was less a stampede than a steady stream. In southern Virginia, enslaved men and women had been escaping to Union-controlled Fortress Monroe since General Butler declared James Townsend, Shepard Mallory, and Frank Baker contraband-of-war and granted asylum to women and children. Within months of the decree, Charles Wilder, superintendent of the contrabands, estimated that ten thousand or more African Americans had made their way to his camps. Those who had arrived in the early months of the war had fled local plantations. In recent months, however, they had traveled long distances, "from Richmond and 200 miles off in North Carolina." Many of them, Wilder claimed, "knew all about the Proclamation and they started on the belief in it."[10]

Black men and women fleeing slavery often found sanctuary in contraband camps set up by the government and supervised by men such as Wilder. At their best, such facilities could ensure a successful transition from slavery to freedom by encouraging independence. A camp just outside of Washington, D.C., on the grounds of Robert E. Lee's confiscated Arlington, Virginia, estate was one of the better equipped and managed of such facilities. Freedmen's Village at its height housed more than a thousand residents and had more than fifty dwellings (each one and a half stories high, divided down the middle and occupied by two families), a hospital, a school, a chapel, and several shops where black men were trained in carpentry and the blacksmith trade and where women were taught sewing. Parks that were named after prominent Union generals and government officials enhanced the community, which had a neat, orderly layout of buildings.[11] The camp established by Union general Grenville Dodge in Corinth, Mississippi (located in the northeastern section of the state), was similar to Freedmen's Village in that it could boast of substantial dwellings, a hospital, a school, and a church. More than six thousand freed people from Alabama and Tennessee, as well as from Mississippi, called the camp home for the brief time that it existed and began their transition to independence.

At their worst, contraband camps made survival tenuous. Most of them were overcrowded and squalid centers of suffering and death, where disease, starvation, and exposure to the cold took a heavy toll and demoralized a people who had believed that their lives would be instantly transformed by freedom. In the summer of 1862, Harriet Jacobs reported from Duff Green's Row—a dilapidated collection of buildings that had been given over to the contrabands in Washington, D.C.—that men, women, and children were "all huddled together without any distinction or regard to age or sex." Jacobs, who knew something about suffering herself (while enslaved she had been forced to hide in an attic for several years before making her way to freedom), found the condition of these men and women "most pitiable." Many had only "a few filthy rags to lie on" or nothing but the bare floor. Others, stricken with "measles, diphtheria, scarlet and typhoid fever," were too weak to care for themselves.[12] Those contrabands in the camps farther south fared no better. At Davis Bend, Mississippi, thirty-five residents of the camp had to huddle together to keep warm, with only "two old quilts and a soldier's old worn out blanket" to share. Firewood had to be carried from a distance of half a mile, and the trek to acquire drinking water was no better.[13] The inadequacy of government support forced camp residents to rely on the philanthropy of northerners who supplied clothing, blankets, and other goods. Elizabeth Keckly (or Keckley), Mrs. Lincoln's modiste and a woman who had purchased her freedom from slavery before the war, founded the Contraband Relief Association in 1862 and urged African Americans to contribute to the care of the freed people. Mrs. Lincoln donated two hundred dollars to the association's fund when it was first established, and she and the president made "frequent contributions" thereafter.[14]

While the contrabands taxed the ability of the Union to provide for them, they offered valuable service in return. Those who had reached Union lines during the first two years of war had been utilized as military laborers; they had thrown up breastworks and fortifications, driven wagons, tended to the sick, and performed all those duties that freed white soldiers for combat. A few of the women found employment as laundresses and cooks. Fugitives also had provided intelligence concerning the whereabouts and strength of the Confederate forces. Women as well as men guided Union troops through Confederate territory or served as spies.[15] Harriet Tubman, the famed Underground Railroad conductor, may have been the most celebrated of the black scouts, but she was by no means alone in her service to the Union.

Black men and women continued to provide such services after the proclamation was issued, but it was the conversion of black men from laborers to soldiers that most benefited the North, and it was from these contraband camps that many were recruited for the Union cause. Gathered into units as U.S. Colored Troops, they were approximately one hundred thousand strong by the end of 1863.[16] By the time the war was over, they had seen combat in more than four hundred battles—thirty-nine of them major ones—including campaigns at Port Hudson, Louisiana; at Milliken's Bend near Vicksburg; at Morris Island, South Carolina (the Fort Wagner assault); and at Chaffin's Farm and the Battle of the Crater in Virginia. The 186,000 black men who served in the army—130,000 or nearly two-thirds of whom were from the South—would make up 10 percent of all Union soldiers.[17]

Lincoln initially doubted black men's ability to become effective soldiers. "If we were to arm them," he suggested to the Chicago Christians who had visited him in September 1862, "I fear that in a few weeks the arms would be in the hands of the rebels."[18] His perception of them could not have been more wrong. Black men—whether freeborn, newly emancipated, or free for years—had longed for the opportunity to prove that they were men, worthy of the same respect as all others. If slavery had taught those recently freed to cower in the presence of white men, the war gave them the opportunity to stand tall. If in freedom some had been denied the pride that came with accomplishment, they hoped that a grateful nation would elevate them when they returned home victorious.

Their path to realizing their aspirations would be neither easy nor swift. They soon discovered that white men who hated slavery often also despised the institution's victims and all who were connected to their class by blood and heritage. They found that some northern men volunteered to command black troops not because they sympathized with the black man's desire to liberate himself and his race but because it afforded an opportunity for the white commanders to advance. Infected with the same racial bigotry that consumed their brothers and sisters in the Confederate South, these men were certain of their moral and intellectual superiority over those they commanded and equally sure that they had to command with a forceful hand. There were many exceptions, of course. When Robert Gould Shaw of Massachusetts took command of the Fifty-Fourth Massachusetts Infantry, he had expressed concern about the abilities of his men and doubted that they would ever see combat. He eventually came to respect them and to appreciate the sacrifices they had made to enter military service. When he fell with them in the assault on Battery Wagner in South Carolina, the Confederates sought to dishonor him by burying him in a common grave with the black soldiers. Knowing how much he had cared about his command, though, his family declined to remove his body after the war ended.

Federal policy regarding black soldiers tended to mirror the unfair perception that they were inferior and unworthy of being treated as equals of white soldiers. Black men had been assured during recruitment that "in respect to pay, equipments, bounty, or aid and protection," they would be treated just as other men, as "soldiers of the Union—nothing less and nothing different."[19] But once mustered in, they discovered that their pay was substantially lower than that of white soldiers, disciplinary action sometimes took the form of flogging as in the days of slavery, and the government was initially not prepared to protect them from Confederates bent on treating black men in Union uniform as if they were "slaves in insurrection," subject to execution, reenslavement, or sale.

Concern for the welfare of black soldiers prompted Frederick Douglass, whose own sons—Charles and Lewis—were serving with the Fifty-Fourth Massachusetts Infantry, to seek a meeting with Lincoln in August 1863. An uncharacteristically apprehensive Douglass arrived at the White House on a typically busy day and immediately had his fears allayed by the president's "kind cordiality and respectful reserve." Douglass outlined three concerns: the pay disparity for black soldiers, the unequal treatment accorded black men when captured by the Confederates, and the failure to promote soldiers who had distinguished themselves in battle. The president advised patience, suggesting that it would take time for Americans to accept the idea of black men shouldering arms and that ultimately justice would prevail. He disagreed with Douglass's argument that the Union should retaliate in kind for the abuse of black men who had been captured. Douglass left the meeting not quite satisfied with Lincoln's reply but impressed with the president's demeanor and his concern for the soldiers.[20] The issues Douglass raised were eventually addressed; black men received equal pay, and Lincoln threatened to retaliate for the abuse of black soldiers by the Confederate forces.

Despite the injustices they faced while in military service, by the summer of 1863 black soldiers had distinguished themselves in battle, prompting Lincoln to declare, "So far as tested, it is difficult to say they are not as good soldiers as any."[21] Lincoln relied on the opinions of his commanders in the field that "the use of colored troops constitute the heaviest blow yet dealt to the rebellion and that, at least one of those important successes, could not have been achieved when it was, but for the aid of black soldiers."[22] Their bravery and devotion to the cause of freedom and union earned them sixteen Congressional Medals of Honor and Lincoln's private and public acknowledgment of their worth.

From the perspective of those enslaved, the most notable service black soldiers rendered during the war was as an army of liberation. The white man's nightmare come true, the armed black men were greeted as near-gods by the enslaved masses. The confident and authoritative demeanor of the men in blue swelled the pride of many a black man, woman, and child. The liberated stood by utterly amazed as black soldiers entered defeated cities or passed through their communities, where on occasion they took the time to destroy the symbols of the slaveholder's power.[23] It was little wonder why young men, eager to cast off servitude, flocked to the northern army.

Andrew Evans was one such youth. Evans had run away before the proclamation was issued but had been returned to his owner. Although enslaved in Missouri, another exempted state, he had greeted the proclamation as if it applied to him. He and his compatriots decided that "the only thing for us to do was to join the Union army and fight for the man who had done so much for us." Initially Evans was rejected because of his age. Undeterred, he traveled to Illinois, where he joined the Seventeenth U.S. Colored Infantry.[24]

For every enslaved person who fled the plantation or joined the Union forces, however, many more chose to stay close to the familiar surroundings of home. Unless the liberating army came through, the perils of flight dissuaded a great number from making the attempt. Those who would be free had to elude both civilian and military patrols as well as lawless, marauding bands of men (both black and white) who took advantage of the chaos of war to terrorize the local populations. The practice of refugeeing also removed many from the opportunity to flee to Union lines. As news of the army's approach reached the farms and plantations, disloyal slaveholders removed themselves and their most valuable property beyond freedom's reach. Discouraging even more enslaved people was uncertainty regarding the northern soldiers' intentions. Planters had spun convincing tales of "Yankee devils" who would carry them away to an unknown hell more terrible than they could imagine. At best, enslaved men and women could expect to be sold and "sent off to Cuba" or "whipped . . . just as in slavery."[25]

The reports of those who fled the plantations but who returned within weeks disillusioned by the experience tended to confirm some parts of their masters' warnings and did not boost enslaved people's confidence in the northern soldiers. Those returnees often told of the horrors of the concentration camps and complained of mistreatment at the hands of white Union troops. Abuse was employed especially against men who refused to enlist in the military. It was common practice in certain areas for black men who resisted the pressures to join to be hunted down and forcibly enrolled. Black men who resisted recruitment efforts often did so at the urging of wives who worried about how families would survive (both financially and physically) once their men were gone. Others doubtless desired to test the freedom that they so cherished and decided that a military life would not afford them that opportunity.

The men and women who remained on the plantations contributed to the overthrow of slavery in their own way. While they continued to provide the labor the Confederacy needed to wage war, including cultivation of cash crops and foodstuffs and work on military fortifications when impressed into service, wartime circumstances slowly transformed attitudes and relationships. Charles Wilder had noted that those men and women entering the Union lines in Virginia "were not afraid of the slaveholders. They said there was nobody on the plantations but women and they were not afraid of them."[26]

Impertinence and defiance became almost commonplace, especially when Union troops were present or nearby. Slave owners complained that laborers who had always behaved in a respectful, deferential manner now grew sullen, disobeyed orders, and refused to accept punishment. In some areas, laborers entered the fields when they wished or absented themselves from work at will.

Lincoln's proclamation had directed the freed people to "abstain from all violence, unless in necessary self-defense," and for the most part, they did. With the exception of an occasional ransacking of the house of a former owner who had fled the Union advance, black men and women declined to exact the retribution that the slaveholders had feared. But not all remained quiet on the southern front. In Mississippi, residents reported that "marauding bands" of "freed negroes" were "desolating neighborhoods" and murdering people in their homes.[27] Both the Confederate military and civilians were certain that they were about to witness a massive revolt of the enslaved population. "We are invaded north, south, and west by a vindictive foe," Governor Charles Clark complained. Clark warned that compromise with the Union would lead to racial equality as well as to the loss of enslaved labor when immediate emancipation was implemented. He preferred to see every young man "sacrificed on the battlefield" and the mass suicide of the remaining men, women, and children rather than the South's social and economic institutions altered by the North.[28]

Even in areas exempted by the proclamation, enslaved men and women challenged the status quo. In Terrebonne Parish, Louisiana, desperate planters complained to Union major general Nathaniel Banks that black men "quit work, go & come when they see fit— Ride off at night the mules that have been at work all day—Fences are pulled down gates & bars are left open—Cattle, & sheep hogs & poultry are killed or carried off & sold—Negroes in numbers go from one plantation to another at all hours night & day—They travel the rail road—They congregate in large numbers on deserted plantations. . . . In a word we are in a State of anarchy."[29]

That African Americans were following their own agenda is evident from activities in Ascension Parish as well. In August 1863, military officials reporting from Donaldsonville complained that several government plantations were controlled by scores of unsupervised black men who were destitute and idle. They had acquired horses and mules and purportedly rode through the countryside threatening local whites and committing crimes. And in the winter of 1863–64, Major General Lovell H. Rousseau, commanding in the District of Nashville, reported that slavery was "virtually dead" in the state, despite its exemption from the provisions of the Emancipation Proclamation. "Many straggling negroes have arms obtained from soldiers, and by their insolence and threats greatly alarm and intimidate white families." Lovell indicated that freedmen left their homes to work for themselves, but returned at night "defiantly asserting their rights to do it."[30]

Occasionally a freedman or freedwoman availed himself or herself of the opportunity to dispense justice on the person responsible for past misdeeds and oppression. Such was the case with the freed laborers of one William Clopton, a notorious Tidewater Virginia planter ("the most cruel slave master in the region") and close friend of former president John Tyler.[31] Clopton had been arrested as a Confederate sympathizer when the Union army entered Charles City County. His capture would have been just another example among many of the neutralizing of a rebel, had the story ended there. But Clopton had a date with destiny. It was his misfortune to be apprehended by the African Brigade, a military unit organized in part with freedmen from Virginia and North Carolina. Some of the men in the unit had been owned by Clopton, and just the day before his capture, three women who had been enslaved by him and who had suffered from his cruelty had found sanctuary with the brigade. At the urging of General Edward Wild, the commanding officer, the women and

William Harris, one of the soldiers, administered a whipping to the elderly man. Harris "played his part conspicuously, bringing the blood from [Clopton's] loins at every stroke, and not forgetting to remind the gentleman of days gone by." The women then took their turn and reminded him "that they were no longer his, but safely housed in Abraham's bosom, and under the protection of the Star Spangled Banner, and guarded by their own patriotic, though once down-trodden race." The irony of the scene did not escape notice. "The day is clear, the fields of grain are beautiful and the birds are singing sweet melodious songs," one observer noted, "while poor Mr. C. is crying to his servants for mercy."[32] General Wild reported that even in their "administration of poetical justice . . . the superior humanity of the Blacks over their white master was manifest in their moderation and backwardness. I wish his back had been as deeply scarred as those of the women, but I abstained and left it to them."[33] The general was later court-martialed for his role in the incident, but the event doubtless left the freed people gratified. The outrage from the local community, however, traveled all the way to the Lincoln White House. Julia Tyler, the widow of the deceased former president, sent a letter to Lincoln protesting Clopton's arrest and beating.[34]

After Lincoln issued the Emancipation Proclamation, "the wind did not blow half so hard as it did before," remembered Richard Parker.[35] Interviewed one year after the war ended, the fifty-eight-year-old minister was still savoring the sweet taste of slavery's demise. For him, freedom was a new experience, yet to be tested by real-life travails. Unfortunately, it did not take most African Americans long to discover the painful truth that freedom did not mean all that they had hoped.

The Emancipation Proclamation swelled the aspirations and broadened the expectations of a people conditioned to imagine little and to expect even less. The president's decree gave the freedmen and freedwomen the opportunity to think beyond the limits imposed by slavery. Hence, as they began to define freedom as the right to equality and fair treatment, their aspirations would clash with the thinking of most southern white men and women. Those who had grown accustomed to controlling a perceived inferior being could hardly have imagined a state of equality with their former property. The freedmen and freedwomen, having been subjected to a lifetime of such control and determined to counter centuries of oppression, could hardly imagine anything else.

Within a year of issuing the proclamation, Lincoln had begun to outline his vision of a reconstructed South free of slavery. Emancipation had been immediate, a situation he had hoped the nation could avoid through gradual emancipation and colonization. That option had been eliminated by his own action and had forced him to consider other possibilities. As early as January 8, just one week after he issued his decree, he hinted at a solution to the problem of immediate emancipation. In a letter to Major General John McClernand, in which he explained that he would not retract the proclamation, he suggested that the Confederate states could protect themselves from the full force of the proclamation by adopting "systems of apprenticeship . . . conforming substantially to the most approved plans of gradual emancipation." If they did this, he argued, they would be "nearly as well off, in this respect, as if the present trouble had not occurred, and much better off than they can possibly be if the contest continues persistently." In the summer of 1863, he indicated to General Nathaniel Banks, commanding in the Department of the Gulf and overseeing the reconstruction of Louisiana, that while he did not presume to influence the state's actions, he hoped that it would adopt a new constitution that recognized the Emancipation Proclamation and that it would free those enslaved people in areas of the state untouched by the decree. In addition, he suggested that Louisiana might want to undergo a "probationary period" to "adopt some practical system by which the two races could gradually live themselves out of their old relation to each other." He expected that the rights of the freed people and the former owners would be protected by fairly executed labor contracts. Doubtless remembering his own nearly nonexistent formal education, Lincoln encouraged the inclusion of education for the black children into the overall scheme. In another letter to General Banks on November 5, the president reiterated his position on freed people, stating that he would not object to Louisiana adopting "a reasonable temporary arrangement, in relation to the landless and homeless freed people," as long as their permanent freedom was not challenged.[36]

By December, Lincoln publicly extended his "suggestions" for Louisiana's reconstruction to include the entire former Confederacy. Clearly, he had not yet given up on the idea of gradualism. "The proposed acquiescence of the national Executive in any reasonable temporary State arrangement for the freed people," he explained in his annual message to Congress, "is made with the view of possibly modifying the confusion and destitution which must, at best, attend all classes by a total revolution of labor throughout whole States." Lincoln believed that southerners would be more inclined to give up slavery if they had control over the process. But he reserved the right to intervene to prevent abuse. As for the border states—those beginning to move in the direction of state emancipation—the president gave his blessings.[37]

Freedmen and freedwomen's idea of freedom differed substantially from what Lincoln was proposing. They agreed with his position on education for black children, and they had no quarrel with labor contracts, as long as they were executed fairly. But a system of apprenticeship was not what they had envisioned. A people eager for independence wanted nothing more than to work for themselves, to own a piece of land, and to live without white interference. In addition, there was an emotional attachment to place as a result of remembered experiences and perceptions that the land was indeed theirs. If, as a Louisiana planter complained, the freed people "believe that the plantations & everything on them belong to them,"[38] it was both because their labor had extracted the wealth from it for white people and because this was home. Fairness dictated, then, that with Union victory and black freedom, the freed people would inherit the land, or at least share it with those who had been responsible for the war.

This was the motivation for a group of black religious leaders who met in January 1865 with Secretary of War Edwin Stanton and Major General William T. Sherman. The twenty men—ranging in age from twenty-six-year-old freeborn James Lynch to seventy-two-year-old freedman Glasgow Taylor—represented the concerns and aspirations of African Americans who inhabited the coastal and Sea Islands areas of South Carolina and Georgia. Nine of them had been freed during the war; only five had never known slavery. Two of the churches represented would have been comparable to the mega-institutions of today, with congregations of twelve hundred and more than eighteen hundred worshippers.

The church leaders selected sixty-seven-year-old Garrison Frazier, who had served in the ministry for thirty-five years, as their official spokesman. Eight years earlier, Frazier had purchased himself and his wife for one thousand dollars in gold and silver. His unsteady health prevented him from currently pastoring a church. Frazier attempted to assure the two Union men of the freed people's loyalty to the federal government and their capacity to provide for themselves. "The way we can best take care of ourselves," he argued, "is to have land, and turn it and till it by our own labor . . . and we can soon maintain ourselves and have something to spare. . . . We want to be placed on land until we are able to buy it and make it our own."[39]

For Frazier and his fellow churchmen, acquisition of land represented the most tangible evidence that they were free, and they did not intend to wait until the war was over to secure it. Aspirations among freedmen and freedwomen for possession of the land that they had worked without compensation increased with the flight of the planters in the face of Union advance. In certain areas of the South—especially the Sea Islands—the government confiscated plantations and farms for nonpayment of the direct tax that had been levied on all of the states to pay for the war.[40] Such lands were subject to sale at public auction, but white investors, primarily from the North, had managed to acquire most of the acreage. Don Carlos Rutter, a freedman who had been cultivating a portion of the land that was now under the control of the government, inquired of the president: "Will you please to be so kind Sir, as to tell me about my little bit of land. I am afraid to put on it a stable, or corn house, and such like, for fear it will be taken away from me again. Will you please to be so kind as to tell me whether the land will be sold from under us or not, or whether it will be sold to us at all." Rutter let the president know that he wanted to purchase the six acres where he had planted cotton, potatoes, and corn. "If we colored people have land I know we shall do very well—there is no fear of that," he asserted confidently. "I had rather work for myself and raise my own cotton than work for a gentleman for wages. . . . Whatever you say I am willing to do, and I will attend to whatever you tell me."⁴¹

A solution came in the form of General Sherman's Special Field Orders No. 15. Although its motivation was not so much inspired by the lament of black farmers as by the general's desire to rid himself of the burden presented by thousands of destitute freed people who had attached themselves to his army, his actions gave them hope. Within a few days of meeting with the black religious leaders, Sherman issued an order declaring that the Sea Islands from Charleston to northern Florida and the abandoned rice fields along the rivers for thirty miles inland would be reserved for settlement by the freed people. Sherman further stipulated that, with the exception of military personnel "detailed for duty," no white persons would be allowed to live on the islands and in the settlements established there. Black people would have complete charge of the areas, limited only by the authority of the U.S. government. Although he directed that the able-bodied be encouraged to enlist in military service, "to contribute their share towards maintaining their own freedom, and securing their rights as citizens of the United States," he warned against attempts to illegally conscript or force black men into the army. Land would be distributed in plots of not more than forty acres, and each head of household would receive "a possessory title."⁴²

Confiscated lands represented hope to a people desperate for independence. But their faith was dashed a few years later, when the original owners were allowed to regain possession. General Oliver Otis Howard, by then director of the Freedmen's Bureau, had the unhappy task of notifying the freedmen and freedwomen of Edisto Island that the lands they thought of as their own would have to be surrendered and that they should make peace with their former masters. "You ask us to forgive the landowners of our island," they responded bitterly in a petition to the Civil War hero. "*You* only lost your right arm in war and might forgive them. The man who tied me to a tree and gave me 39 lashes and who stripped and flogged my mother and my sister and who will not let me stay in his empty hut except I will do his planting and be satisfied with his price and who combines with others to keep away land from me well knowing I would not have anything to do with him if I had land of my own—that man I cannot well forgive."[43]

Most African Americans never got the chance to possess the land, even for a short time. Instead, they labored on government farms or on lands leased, again to northerners and southern white men. Such lands were cultivated by the freed people for wages, but under such arrangements they fared little better than during slavery. In Louisiana, for instance, the system of "free labor" instituted by General Banks allowed freedmen to choose their place of employment but forced them to contract for work for the entire year at that job. Any infractions of the rules (insolence and disobedience, for instance) could result in forfeiture of pay or arrest.

Even in areas exempted by the proclamation, black men and women took advantage of absent owners to cultivate the land on their own. In Terrebonne Parish, Louisiana, the residents of the Potts plantation complained that they had received permission from the provost marshal at Thibodeaux to "cultivate the land on the Plantation, and do something for ourselves," but just as they had prepared the ground and begun to plant, a white man arrived to claim the acres. "We have had a hard struggle to get along," they complained, "and we feel it hard now that we have succeeded in making ourselves in a measure independent, to have to [turn] it all over to someone else." The industriousness of the group, consisting of about sixty people, "a very large proportion" of them "aged men, women & young children," was confirmed by a Treasury Department agent who found that "they have made sufficient Corn for their own use and some to sell. . . . Larger returns will be found from the management of this place than any one I have seen managed by inexperienced Govm't agents or soldiers."[44] His confidence in the ability of the freed people to work independently apparently did not persuade his superiors, as the practice of forcing black men and women into contracts continued throughout and after the war.

If land acquisition symbolized freedom, political rights helped to maintain it. Freed people, the freeborn, and those freed before the war understood that their rights could not be secured without the ability to determine what laws would impact their lives. Indicative of this effort was the petition of black residents of Nashville a few months before the war concluded. After thanking the government for the Emancipation Proclamation, they asked that the state "abolish the last vestige of slavery by the express words of your organic law." They reminded the state that its free black residents had voted for thirty-nine years (1796–1835) and that they had done so without embarrassment. They argued that nearly two hundred thousand black men were currently fighting for preservation of the Union and had thus earned citizenship rights. "The Government has asked the colored man to fight for its preservation and gladly has he done it," the petitioners continued. "It can afford to trust him with a vote as safely as it trusted him with a bayonet."[45]

As black men petitioned local governments, others appealed directly to Lincoln. In early 1864 the president received a petition signed by a thousand black men requesting that they be allowed to register to vote. The men were residents of New Orleans, many of them members of the relatively prosperous free black community. Their wealth and education, the product of generations of freedom and privilege, as a consequence of their intimate connections with white residents of the city, often rivaled that of their white neighbors. Perhaps the president was influenced by their success and what in his estimation would have been their readiness for citizenship. As early as March 1864, when Louisiana was constructing a new government in preparation for returning to the Union, Lincoln had proposed privately that the state might consider giving the vote to certain African Americans. "I barely suggest for your private consideration," he wrote to Michael Hahn, newly elected governor of Louisiana, "whether some of the colored people may not be let in—as, for instance, the very intelligent and especially those who have fought gallantly in our ranks. They would probably help in some trying time to come, to keep the jewel of liberty within the family of freedom."[46] Lincoln cautioned that his idea was meant as a suggestion only, and for Hahn alone.

A year later, just three days prior to his assassination, he made his views public in his last address. Given in the aftermath of Lee's surrender to Grant, and of Louisiana's adoption of a new constitution, the president cautioned that it was better to accept limited progress than to insist on concessions that were not possible at that time. Louisiana had agreed to provide public school education to black children, and the state had authorized the legislature to permit voting rights for black men at some later date. Perhaps as importantly, the state had voted ratification of the Thirteenth Amendment, outlawing slavery throughout the country.[47] For Lincoln, it was about compromise and realistic goals. He believed he had extracted as much as he could from the former Confederate state.

ENDING SLAVERY FOREVER

On January 31, 1865, roughly two years after President Lincoln had declared the enslaved population in the Confederate states free, the House of Representatives approved a bill calling for a constitutional amendment to outlaw slavery in America. From the very beginning, the president and champions of freedom had worried that an emancipating decree based on military necessity might not withstand a legal challenge once the Union was secured. And, of course, there was the matter of what to do with the 830,000 enslaved people who were not touched by the proclamation. Moreover, Lincoln and others desired to prevent slavery from being reinstituted in the former Confederacy once the war was over. Since the issuing of the proclamation, both friends and adversaries had urged him to rescind it, believing that it served to divide the nation even further rather than to provide a solution to the rebellion. He consistently refused to retract it: "the promise being made," he argued, "must be kept."[1] Lincoln's Proclamation of Amnesty and Reconstruction stipulated that former Confederates take an oath of allegiance to the Union and swear to uphold all congressional acts and presidential decrees involving enslaved people as long as they were not repealed or modified by Congress or the Supreme Court. It reflected his commitment to hold firm but also hinted at the potential challenge that his wartime emancipation measure faced.[2]

The political climate and public sentiment in the fourth year of the war encouraged support for an amendment that would exceed the provisions of the Emancipation Proclamation and discourage legal challenges. The horrific loss of life on the battlefield and in the camps had convinced many northerners that the divisiveness caused by slavery's continued presence anywhere in the country was too great a cost. Swayed by the argument that irrevocable universal emancipation was the only solution to preserving the Union and ridding the nation of the potential for such future disagreements, northern residents sent petitions to Congress calling for action. Indicative of this effort was the Women's National Loyal League, which under the leadership of Elizabeth Cady Stanton and Susan B. Anthony collected one hundred thousand signatures and in the winter of 1864 presented them to Radical Republican senator Charles Sumner for delivery to the Senate. By summer, the number of signatures had reached four hundred thousand.[3] And in the border states, growth in the ranks of antislavery Democrats pressed the cause of perpetual freedom for all.

How to implement universal emancipation, however, became the subject of intense debate. Even in the midst of war, there were those, Lincoln included, who believed that such sweeping emancipation remained within jurisdiction of the states. Congress could not lawfully legislate slavery's demise. There were others who saw a solution to the problem in the form of a constitutional amendment. The document that had implicitly protected slavery could now be used to destroy it. Even among the proponents of freedom, however, the ratification of such an amendment was not a foregone conclusion. With the exception of the Bill of Rights, the Constitution had been amended only twice. No new amendment had been ratified since 1804, and many believed it should undergo no additional revision.

Nevertheless, in December 1863, Republican congressman James Ashley of Ohio proposed a bill that would "amend the national Constitution prohibiting slavery, or involuntary servitude, in all of the states and Territories now owned or which may be hereafter acquired by the United States."[4] This was followed by another proposal from Iowa Republican congressman James Wilson. The two bills were submitted to the Judiciary Committee for consideration. When the bill reached the floor, it encountered considerable opposition, primarily from Peace Democrats and representatives from Kentucky. The supporters of the proposed amendment in the House recorded ninety-three votes to the opposition's sixty-five, thus failing to secure the necessary two-thirds majority needed to have it passed.

In the meantime, Missouri senator John Brooks Henderson had introduced a joint resolution to the Senate for a proposed amendment to the Constitution. That Henderson, a senator from a border state, would introduce the bill is testament to the extraordinary transformation in sentiment regarding slavery during the course of the war. In an effort to arrest the secession movement, Lincoln had initially attempted to appease the slaveholding Unionists and later tried to persuade them that slavery within their borders would not survive the "friction of war." He believed the loyalty of Kentucky, especially, was crucial to Union success. The border states' rejection of his argument that they should implement their own policies of emancipation had led him to seek another solution in the form of the Emancipation Proclamation. The federal shift from protection of the right of ownership of human property to emancipation and the use of armed black men in the Union cause had irrevocably affected the exempted states as well. In 1864, two of them—Missouri and Maryland—would heed Lincoln's warning, although too late to benefit from the compensation that had been promised to slaveholders for the loss of their property.

Henderson's bill had been sent to the Senate Judiciary Committee, and on February 10, Senator Lyman Trumbull, chairman of the committee, reported the revised bill, which incorporated features of the several proposals that had been submitted for consideration in both houses of Congress. Absent from the revised bill was a proposal by Senator Charles Sumner that had been more radical than the others in that it aimed to guarantee equality as well as abolish slavery. Sumner's proposal stated, "All persons are equal before the law, so that no person can hold another as a slave." It charged Congress with making "all laws necessary and proper to carry this declaration into effect everywhere in the United States."[5]

The Senate opened debate on the proposed amendment in late March with Senator Trumbull offering a plea for passage. If the amendment was adopted, he argued, "we are forever freed of this troublesome question. We accomplish then what the statesmen of this country have been struggling to accomplish for years. We take this question entirely away from the politics of the country. We relieve Congress of sectional strifes, and, what is better than all, we restore to a whole race that freedom which is theirs by the gift of God, but which we for generations have wickedly denied them."[6] The largely Republican argument in favor of an amendment was strengthened by the support of Democrats such as Reverdy Johnson of Maryland, who gave a powerful speech during the debates in which he urged his fellow legislators to outlaw slavery in order to ensure a "prosperous and permanent peace."[7] When the Senate voted on April 8, it approved the amendment, thirty-eight votes to six.

Support from border state senators and representatives such as Henderson and Johnson did not imply that there was a lessening of objections to extending rights to African Americans. In response to suggestions that abolition would lead to political rights for the newly emancipated, Henderson had argued, "We give [the slave] no right except his freedom, and leave the rest to the States."[8] Of course, few were naive enough to believe that any of the states in the Confederacy (or in the Union slaveholding states, for that matter) would extend any political or social rights to the freed people.

As the debates had unfolded in the House and Senate in early 1864, the president refrained from publicly expressing any opinion on the merits of a constitutional amendment. When Illinois congressman Isaac Arnold pressed him to use the occasion of his annual message to Congress in December 1863 to recommend such an amendment, Lincoln declined, apparently because he continued to favor state-controlled abolition. Two months later, Republican congressman John Defrees of Indiana suggested that he send a message to Congress endorsing an amendment that would prohibit slavery forever. "It would be *your* measure," Defrees stressed. "If not done very soon the proposition *will* be presented by the Democracy[9] and claimed by them as *their* proposition." Lincoln offered a terse reply: "Our own friends have this under consideration now, and will do as much without a Message as with it."[10] He would not offer public support for such an amendment until June, after the Senate had approved the measure and before it fell to defeat in the House.

Aware of the growing northern opposition to slavery and eager to maintain their preeminence as the antislavery party, the Republicans used the occasion of their national convention to remind the electorate that their policies had the best chances for success. While meeting in Baltimore on June 7 and 8 and now calling themselves the National Union Party, they adopted a platform that blamed slavery for the current state of affairs, argued that justice and national safety demanded its destruction, and called for a constitutional amendment that would "terminate and forever prohibit the existence of Slavery within the limits of the jurisdiction of the United States."[11] Despite concern on the part of certain leaders that the president might not be able to win reelection, he was nominated on the first ballot. When notified of his victory, he expressed gratitude for the party's continuing confidence in him and anticipated that he would accept renomination officially after he had read the platform. But for now, he wanted them to know that he approved the party's declaration favoring a constitutional amendment. He recalled that the seceded states had been given one hundred days to return to the Union and had been promised that no harm would come to slavery. When the states had ignored the notice, "such [an] amendment of the Constitution as [is] now proposed, became a fitting, and necessary conclusion to the final success of the Union cause." He urged unconditional Union men everywhere to "give it legal form, and practical effect."[12]

When the Democrats met in convention in Chicago nearly three months later, they ignored the shift in public opinion. Rather than endorse a constitutional amendment, they stressed the alleged misdeeds of the Lincoln administration. The platform declared that the party's aim was to "preserve the Federal Union and the rights of the States unimpaired." It demanded "immediate efforts be made for a cessation of hostilities" and called for the restoration of peace "at the earliest practicable moment . . . on the basis of the Federal Union of the States."[13]

The presidential election was far from won in the summer of 1864. Although opposition from John C. Frémont, nominee of the newly formed Democracy Party, had fizzled, the traditional Democratic Party candidate, former Union general George B. McClellan, remained a serious threat. McClellan was supported by Peace Democrats (although he was not one of them) and by those who believed states' rights should triumph over human rights (at least in regard to African Americans). McClellan's popularity in certain circles and the Union's disastrous failures on the battlefield convinced even Lincoln that Republican defeat was imminent.

It was during this summer before the 1864 election that Lincoln and Frederick Douglass met for the second time, in this instance at Lincoln's initiation. Disappointing Union performance on the battlefield and continuing opposition from Peace Democrats prompted the president to worry that he might be compelled to accept a settlement that would end the war prematurely and forever trap those African Americans declared free by the proclamation behind Confederate lines. The president requested that the former bondman help to devise a plan to inform those in the Confederacy of the Emancipation Proclamation's existence and to facilitate their escape. Although Douglass agreed, Union victories in succeeding weeks and congressional approval of an abolition amendment rendered such a plan unnecessary.[14]

But if Douglass was impressed by Lincoln's commitment to black freedom, not all African Americans concurred. In the 1864 election, there were those who chose to support others, such as Frémont, whose Democracy Party platform had included support for a constitutional amendment that both ended slavery *and* ensured equality for all. Before Frémont had left the race, a soldier of the Fifty-Fourth Massachusetts offered an argument for why Lincoln was problematic as a candidate for reelection. "Many of our intelligent colored men believe in Mr. Lincoln; but we, who have studied him thoroughly, know him better." The soldier's criticism was predicated on what he viewed as Lincoln's "fickle-minded" policy in regard to emancipation and black advancement. He was judged "one who, holding anti-slavery principles in one hand and colonization in the other, always gave concessions to slavery when the *Union* could be preserved without touching the peculiar institution. Such a man is not again worthy the votes of the voting portion of the colored race, when the intrepid Frémont . . . the well-known freedom-cherishing, negro-equalizing patriot, is the competitor." The soldier "thanked" the president "for what the exigencies of the times forced him to do" and criticized him for not taking full advantage of the opportunities the war presented.[15] When the votes were cast, however, many soldiers supported the president and helped him to win reelection. Of the twenty-five states whose residents cast ballots, McClellan won only three.

With the election behind him, Lincoln turned his attention to the House of Representatives, where the debate over the Thirteenth Amendment was again underway. The struggle in the House differed significantly from what had transpired in the Senate one year earlier. While the Republicans dominated the latter, the party's numerical strength was not as great in the House, where 102 Republicans sat among 75 Democrats. Nevertheless, Lincoln proposed that the current members—who had already voted the bill down in June—reconsider before the new Congress convened. The fight was intense, both on the floor of the House chamber and privately, where supposedly certain representatives were persuaded to vote in favor of the amendment in exchange for political favors and possibly other considerations. Whether these were offered with the knowledge and approval of the president is uncertain. What *is* certain, however, is that Lincoln expended considerable political capital in his effort to get the amendment passed. His decision to remain silently in the shadows when the measure was making its way through the Senate and in its first journey through the House was now replaced by a resolve to get the job done.

In the House, Congressman Ashley maneuvered his fellow representatives toward a favorable vote. Among the representatives to speak in favor of passage was Thaddeus Stevens of Pennsylvania. The ardent abolitionist delivered an impassioned speech that reflected many years of service to the cause of freedom. "We have suffered for slavery more than all the plagues of Egypt," he declared. "We still harden our hearts, and refuse to let the people go."[16] Stevens warned that until proslavery men yielded to God's command and the demands of humanity and voted for abolition, the scourge of slavery would remain. In the end, the vote, taken on January 31, 1865, stood at 119 for and 56 against, thus barely securing the necessary two-thirds majority. Although not required to do so, Lincoln signed the measure on February 1 and sent it on to the states for ratification. The first to do so was Illinois; and at the end of the year, on December 6, 1865, Georgia supplied the required number to make the amendment a part of the Constitution. Several states ratified after the requisite number had been reached. Three of them—Delaware, Kentucky, and Mississippi—ratified the amendment in 1901, 1976, and 1995, respectively. Mississippi has the dubious distinction of not making official notification of ratification until 2013!

The passage of the Thirteenth Amendment by the House of Representatives did not elicit the emotional response evidenced by the Emancipation Proclamation. Perhaps it was because Americans found it somewhat premature, since the required number of states would have to ratify it before it became law. But neither was it ignored. Within days of its passage by Congress, Henry Highland Garnet was invited to deliver a sermon celebrating the event in the House chamber. Garnet, then the pastor of the Fifteenth Street Presbyterian Church in the District of Columbia, thus became the first African American to speak in the capitol building. Titled "Let the Monster Perish," his sermon outlined the destructiveness of slavery to the nation ("It has wasted the treasure of the Commonwealth and the lives of thousands of brave men") and enumerated its sins against the bondmen and bondwomen (it "attempts to make a man a brute. It treats him as a beast"). While he was pleased that Congress had "saved succeeding generations from the guilt of oppression, and from the wrath of God," he declared that the struggle was not yet over. The champion of freedom could rest only "when all unjust and heavy burdens shall be removed from every man in the land. When all invidious and proscriptive distinctions shall be blotted out from our laws. . . . When emancipation shall be followed by enfranchisement, and all men holding allegiance to the government shall enjoy every right of American citizenship." Garnet reminded his audience that black soldiers, while sacrificing themselves on the field of battle, were denied the right to a political voice and could not expect promotion to the higher ranks.[17]

Frederick Douglass responded similarly a few months later on the occasion of the thirty-second annual meeting of the American

Anti-Slavery Society. In response to the argument of some that the society should disband because its work had been done, Douglass suggested, "[W]hether this Constitutional Amendment is law or not . . . I hold that the work of the Abolitionists is not done. . . . The South by unfriendly legislation, could make our liberty, under that provision, a delusion, a mockery, and a snare." Douglass argued that until the black man had secured the vote, could testify in a court of law, and had received the right to bear arms, "slavery is not abolished."[18]

On March 4, the president delivered his second inaugural address. He began his remarks with reference to the previous inaugural address, when the nation had verged on a civil war. Although both sides sought to avert it, he declared, the war came. Lincoln then turned his attention to the central theme. He suggested that the cause of the war was the "peculiar and powerful interest" in the southern states in the form of enslaved people and the desire of those states to "strengthen, perpetuate, and extend" the slaveholding interest. But he declined to vilify the South or to hold it singly responsible for the war. Instead, he chose to emphasize the common bonds between the two sections. "Both read the same Bible, and pray to the same God, and each invokes His aid against the other." And if some thought it strange that anyone should ask God's assistance in exploiting the labor of another, Lincoln cautioned them to "judge not that we be not judged." He saw the war as a burden shared equally by North and South as atonement for black bondage. "Fondly do we hope— fervently do we pray," he continued, that the war would end soon. But if it was God's will that it continue until "all the wealth piled by the bond-man's two hundred and fifty years of unrequited toil shall be sunk, and until every drop of blood drawn with the lash, shall be paid by another drawn with the sword," the American people would have to endure it. Lincoln ended this brief but arguably the most powerful of his addresses with a charge to all to move forward without hatred and recrimination and to honor the debt they owed to those who had sacrificed themselves on the battlefield.[19] He called for an America of unity and brotherhood "with malice toward none" and "charity for all," where old antagonisms would be resolved and "a just, and a lasting peace" would prevail.

Later that evening, Frederick Douglass made his way to the White House where the inaugural reception was underway. Fully aware that his presence would likely be received with disdain by celebrants, he nevertheless approached the door and sought admission. When two policemen refused to admit him on the grounds that they were ordered to keep people of color away, Douglass protested that the newly reelected president would never have sanctioned such behavior. As providence would have it, a passerby observed the incident and accepted Douglass's request to inform Lincoln of what was transpiring. Upon Lincoln's intervention Douglass was admitted. The president greeted his guest cordially and asked him what he thought of the inaugural address. "Mr. Lincoln, that was a sacred effort," Douglass assured him.[20] Gone were the years of criticism and doubt. In their place was a hope-filled anticipation of better times to come. The former bondman left the reception doubtless believing that this second term of the Lincoln administration would bring to his people the freedom they had envisioned.

EPILOGUE

B y the end of the year, America was free, at least under the law. Slavery had been removed from the nation's fields, factories, homes, and public places by a constitutional amendment that outlawed one person's ownership of another. The nation, indivisible, was working its way back to a fervently hoped-for lasting peace. Tragically, destiny, in the guise of John Wilkes Booth, would rob the president of the opportunity to experience this free and united America. Thus was born the iconic Lincoln, the selfless leader who was snatched from his beloved nation at the moment of his triumph.

The mourning rituals for the martyred president presaged the position he would occupy in national memory. In Victorian-era fashion, Americans draped their homes and public buildings in black cloth, women wore official mourning attire, and men donned black armbands fashioned from crepe. Sentiments of sorrow and anger poured in to newspapers, as Americans grappled with this deeply personal and national tragedy. In a series of dispatches from Washington, the *New York Herald* kept its readers informed of what was transpiring in the capital. In one of its reports the newspaper described the despondent atmosphere: "Flags over the departments and throughout the city are at half mast. Scarcely any business is being transacted anywhere, either in private or public account. Our citizens, without any preconcert whatever, are draping their premises with festoons of mourning. The bells are tolling mournfully. All is the deepest gloom and sadness. Strong men weep in the streets. The grief is widespread and deep, and in strange contrast to the joy so lately manifested over our recent military victories. This is indeed a day of gloom."[1]

As Lincoln lay in state in the White House on April 18, mourners thronged the streets and avenues, impeding regular traffic. Americans from diverse backgrounds and ideologies, "old and young, rich and poor—all sexes, grades and colors," lined up for the opportunity to file past his body and to silently express their regard for the man and the leader. By the end of the day, at least thirty thousand mourners had paid their respects. Among those who came was a group of wounded soldiers who were currently resident in the local hospitals. Wearing the scars of battle, they said their final farewells to the man who many regarded as "Father Abraham."[2]

Washington was joined in its public mourning by the rest of the country, especially so in those places touched by the train that bore Lincoln's body to its final resting place in Springfield, Illinois. As it passed through one community after another, the people gathered along the sides of the tracks or lined up to pay their respects in those places where the funeral train stopped. In the days and weeks that followed, thousands of resolutions and expressions of sorrow were sent from around the world. Sermons were preached in Lincoln's honor, and speakers pledged to complete his work.

The president's death fell especially hard on the African American population. Of course, they shared the nation's loss, but their grief reflected much more than the passing of a leader. Many in the African American community recognized in Lincoln someone who had opened the door of freedom for them and who they expected would champion their right to full inclusion in American society. If the nation had lost a great statesman, many black men and women believed they had lost a benefactor and a friend.

From the North to the Lower South, black men and women expressed their grief collectively in public gatherings and individually and privately in letters written to friends and acquaintances. In Bloomington, Illinois, black residents of the city met at a local church where they mourned "a *tried friend*—A GREAT DELIVERER—A REAL BENEFACTOR." Those assembled resolved "to aid the government *by every means* in the destruction of the monster slavery, looking forward to, and praying for the day when the jubilee of freedom shall be proclaimed throughout the land, and the American flag shall cease to wave o'er slaves!" In San Francisco thousands marched through the streets and gathered at a local church to hear their leaders pay tribute to Lincoln.[3] In the South freedmen and freedwomen observed the president's passing with even greater solemnity. In New Orleans ten thousand residents representing dozens of benevolent and fraternal orders congregated at Congo Square, where they agreed to observe a thirty-day period of mourning.[4]

Given Lincoln's significance to the African American community, it seemed fitting that they would be among the first to erect a monument in his honor. Barely a month after the assassination, Major Martin Delany of the 104th Regiment of the U.S. Colored Troops (one of fewer than a hundred black field grade officers) proposed that every black man, woman, and child contribute at least one cent to build a national monument honoring the martyred president.[5] Delany had hoped that the structure could be erected in Illinois, near the president's family home. While he did not get his choice of location, funds were secured for another monument, this one to be located in the District of Columbia. Legend has it that the first five dollars were contributed by Charlotte Scott, a freedwoman who had pledged her "first earnings in freedom" when she heard the news of Lincoln's assassination.[6] The famous Thomas Ball sculpture, paid for primarily by freed people like Scott but designed without the input of African Americans, elicited criticism then and now for its depiction of a half-kneeling black man being summoned to rise by a towering "emancipator." Frederick Douglass suggested that the image conveyed dependence, "when a more manly attitude would have been indicative of freedom."[7]

How ironic that this effort of the freed people to honor Lincoln began, not with someone who had been liberated by the Emancipation Proclamation, but with a freedwoman who had been released from bondage roughly one year before Lincoln issued the decree. In 1862 Scott's owner had been forced to flee Confederate Virginia because of his Union sympathies. The family had settled in Ohio, taking Scott along with them. Now free, she chose—perhaps out of necessity because of her advanced age (for that time, at least) or perhaps out of some misdirected sense of loyalty—to stay with those who had kept her in bondage for nearly sixty-two years.

Purportedly, Scott had greeted the news of Lincoln's assassination with the assertion that "the colored people have lost their best friend on earth."[8] Many African Americans would have joined her in that assessment. That regard for Lincoln was evident in early April 1865 when, accompanied by his young son Tad, the president entered the defeated Confederate capital at Richmond. J. J. Hill, an orderly with the Twenty-Ninth Connecticut Colored Infantry, reported what he had witnessed on that extraordinary day: "As the President passed along the street the colored people waved their handkerchiefs, hats and bonnets, and expressed their gratitude by shouting repeatedly, 'Thank God for his goodness; we have seen his salvation . . .' They were earnest and heartfelt expressions of gratitude to Almighty God, and thousands of colored men in Richmond would have laid down their lives for President Lincoln. . . . The gratitude and admiration amounting almost to worship, with which the colored people of Richmond received the President must have deeply touched his heart."[9]

Speaking at Cooper Union within weeks of Lincoln's death, Frederick Douglass indicated that "no class of people . . . have a better reason for lamenting the death of Abraham Lincoln . . . than have the colored people." Douglass considered him "emphatically the black man's president." He summarized all that African Americans had experienced under the Lincoln administration: freedom, recognition of Haitian and Liberian independence, and black advancement. Most of all, slavery was destroyed forever. "Henceforth," Douglass declared, "an American citizen may defend his country without defending a scandalous crime."[10]

Despite such heartfelt words and in spite of monuments erected in his memory, the African American regard for Lincoln revealed complexity from the very beginning of his martyrdom. Eleven years after Douglass made his impassioned speech in the Cooper Union eulogy, he delivered another that was less laudatory. The occasion was the dedication of Charlotte Scott's *Freedmen's Memorial*. In attendance were President Ulysses S. Grant, cabinet members, Supreme

Court justices, and members of Congress, all doubtless waiting to hear the man who had been born into slavery pay homage to the "Great Emancipator." Douglass did not shrink from the task, although his remarks could hardly have been acceptable to all in attendance. The great orator and abolitionist declared that Lincoln "was not, in the fullest sense of the word, either our man or our model. In his interests, in his associations, in his habits of thought, and in his prejudices, he was a white man." In Douglass's estimation, Lincoln was "preeminently the white man's President, entirely devoted to the welfare of white men." What followed was a candid critique of the president's actions in the first years of the war: the return of would-be self-emancipators to their rebel owners; his colonization scheme; his stated willingness to save the Union at the expense of black freedom, if need be; his initial rejection of black soldiers; his revocation of Frémont's proclamation freeing enslaved people in Missouri. "He was ready and willing at any time during the first years of his administration," Douglass reminded, "to deny, postpone, and sacrifice the rights of humanity in the colored people to promote the welfare of the white people of this country. . . . You are the children of Abraham Lincoln. We are at best only his step-children; children by adoption, children by forces of circumstances and necessity." Yet, Douglass acknowledged the African American debt to Lincoln in helping to break the chains of bondage. "[T]hough the Union was more to him than our freedom or our future, under his wise and beneficent rule we saw ourselves gradually lifted from the depths of slavery to the heights of liberty and manhood."[11]

Despite the obvious ambivalence in some circles, the Lincoln image in the African American community was perpetuated by annual emancipation celebrations that kept the promise of the Emancipation Proclamation alive. Most members of the community celebrated Emancipation Day on January 1, but others designated their own special day that reflected when their particular community either learned about or actually acquired their freedom. For instance, Richmond, Virginia, residents commemorated emancipation on April 3, the day in 1865 when Union troops seized the city from the Confederate government. In 1866 black citizens of West Chester, Pennsylvania, celebrated the fourth anniversary of the proclamation on September 22, as did the residents of West Grove, the day Lincoln introduced the preliminary decree.[12] In July 1865 the residents of Augusta, Georgia, celebrated Independence Day and Emancipation Day simultaneously. The "Freedmen's Celebration" featured Reverend James Lynch, a noted minister of the African Methodist Episcopal Church, who "paid a most glowing tribute to the memory" of Lincoln.[13]

Emancipation Day celebrations generally included widespread participation from area residents who enjoyed the parades, sang uplifting songs, and listened to spirited orations. Such gatherings provided a platform for the continuing struggle for civil and political rights. In that regard, the events were as political as they were celebratory. Participants reminded their audiences that equality was not yet won and that they had an obligation to continue to restructure America along the lines that Lincoln had intended.

Less focused on civil and political rights than on opportunities for earning a living and securing the goodwill of southern white men, Booker T. Washington, the master of accommodation, redefined Lincoln's great accomplishment. In a speech he delivered to the Republican Club of New York on the hundredth anniversary of Lincoln's birthday, Washington emphasized the liberation from spiritual bondage that white men and women had enjoyed as a consequence of the president's signing the Emancipation Proclamation. The proclamation was "a great event . . . and yet it was but the symbol of another, still greater and more momentous. . . . The same pen that gave freedom to four millions of African slaves at the same time struck the shackles from the souls of twenty-seven millions of Americans of another color." In freeing the enslaved, Lincoln freed America and set an example for the rest of the world. In addition, he served as a worldwide symbol to the downtrodden and to those who rose from humble beginnings. If Lincoln could do it, so could African Americans. Washington ended his address by praising the white men of the South and by reminding his audience of Lincoln's patience and his refusal to express animus toward those who disagreed with him.[14]

Of course, not everyone agreed with Washington, especially with his emphasis on economic advancement over all things. On the fiftieth anniversary of the Emancipation Proclamation, Alexander Walters, bishop of the African Methodist Episcopal Zion Church, invoked Lincoln's name in a different way. While Washington had remained silent on the issue of civil and political rights, Walters urged black men and women to continue the struggle. "I have no sympathy with that class of leaders who are advising the Negro to eschew politics in deference to color prejudice," he declared. "If we would properly honor [Lincoln] we must finish the work which he so nobly began— the lifting up of the Negro race to the highest point of civilization."[15]

The seventy-fifth anniversary of the Emancipation Proclamation saw the ranks of the freedmen and freedwomen dwindling as old age and poverty took their toll. The freed people's memories of slavery had been dulled by the passage of time and by the conditions under which they lived. Some of those who had felt the promise of the proclamation as they started their new lives in freedom now questioned Lincoln's commitment to their liberation. They compared the Great Depression's austere living with their lives under bondage and found the former wanting by comparison. Much of the dissatisfaction centered on the failure of Lincoln and the government to secure an economic independence for the people whom he freed. Henri Necaise complained that "[they] went and turned us loose, just like a passel of cattle, and didn't show us nothin' or give us nothin'. [There] was acres and acres of land not in use, and lots of timber in dis country. [They] should a give each one of us a little farm and let us get out timber and build houses."[16] Similarly, Thomas Hall's postemancipation experiences had left him bitter and critical of the man who was credited with his freedom. "Lincoln got the praise for freeing us, but did he do it?" Hall questioned. "He give us freedom without giving us any chance to live to ourselves and we still had to depend on the southern white man for work, food and clothing, and he held us through our necessity and want in a state of servitude but little better than slavery. Lincoln done but little for the negro race and from a living standpoint nothing."[17] When asked what he thought of Lincoln, Jacob Thomas responded sarcastically that he had "always thought a lot of Lincoln 'cause he had a heap of faith in de [black man] ter think dat he could live on nothin' at all."[18]

But not all viewed Lincoln so disparagingly. Although the reverence of the postemancipation era had faded, some former bondmen continued to remember Lincoln fondly. Many would have agreed with William Henry Towns, an eighty-four-year-old Alabama freedman. "Some say that Abe wasn't interested so much in freein' the slaves as he was in savin' the Union," Towns suggested. "Don't make no difference, he sho' done a big thing. . . . Any man that tries to help humanity is a good man."[19] Perhaps many felt like Sallie Paul of Marion, South Carolina. When asked what she thought about Lincoln, she replied: "I ain't took time to have no thoughts bout him. . . . Hear talk dat he been de one dat free de slaves, but who de power? . . . God set de slaves free. De Lord do it. Abraham Lincoln couldn' do no more den what God give de power to do."[20]

As Lincoln faded in the memory and the hearts of the freedmen and freedwomen, their children and grandchildren learned that he could still serve as a powerful symbol. Hence, in 1939, when noted contralto Marian Anderson was refused the use of Constitution Hall by the Daughters of the American Revolution, the National Association for the Advancement of Colored People suggested that the Lincoln Memorial be secured instead. With the assistance of Eleanor Roosevelt and the permission of the president, Anderson gave an Easter Sunday concert that attracted seventy-five thousand people, with millions more tuning in to the NBC Radio broadcast. In his introduction of Anderson, Secretary of the Interior Harold Ickes signaled the significance of the moment and the venue. "It is appropriate that we stand reverently and humbly at the base of this memorial to the great emancipator while glorious tribute is rendered to his memory by a daughter of the race from which he struck the chains of slavery." The symbol of Lincoln's commitment to black equality was thus transferred to the memorial that bore his name.[21]

Two years later, A. Philip Randolph proposed a "March on Washington" that would have ended at the memorial had he not been able to persuade President Roosevelt to listen to his demands that African Americans be assured equal access to government jobs. In 1957 the Prayer Pilgrimage for Freedom used the memorial as its backdrop while reminding Americans that people of color still suffered from segregation and unequal access to the voting polls. And in the 1963 March on Washington for Jobs and Freedom, Dr. Martin Luther King Jr. began his address with a reference to Lincoln and the Emancipation Proclamation, a "momentous decree" that "came as a great beacon light of hope to millions of Negro slaves who had been seared in the flames of withering injustice." He reminded those assembled that true freedom—the absence of segregation and discrimination—remained unrealized.[22]

After a century and a half, Lincoln continues to serve as a gauge by which to assess Americans' progress. On November 4, 2008, the nation witnessed what many saw as the embodiment of his legacy. Barack Obama, a man not descended from enslaved people but whose African ancestry has shaped his experience in America, became the nation's forty-fourth president. Given the general disregard for people of color in his time, it is doubtful that Lincoln could have imagined such a thing occurring. But his actions 150 years ago helped to make it a possibility. In his initial campaign and throughout his administration, President Obama has invoked Lincoln's name and memory, reminding Americans of the legacy of inclusion and of opportunity that the proclamation and its author symbolized. Like Lincoln, he has faced the challenges of a divided nation and has struggled to get his vision of America accepted by the majority of its people.

* * *

Twenty months into the war, Lincoln had proclaimed freedom for over three million enslaved people and had destroyed their legal status as chattel. The Thirteenth Amendment, ratified nearly three years later, freed all who remained in bondage and guaranteed that the institution could not be reconstituted. But neither proclamation nor constitutional amendment ensured the equality of opportunity and fair treatment that the freedmen and freedwomen and their prewar free brothers and sisters had envisioned. That would come after a century of struggle.

The quest for full inclusion in American society had not begun with Lincoln's proclamation; black men and women had agitated for their rights even before the nation as citizens now know it had been conceived. And they continued to do so in the aftermath of emancipation. The proclamation served as a reminder of the nation's implied promise to those who had been denied the rights espoused in its founding documents. If the Declaration of Independence and the Constitution had not explicitly included black people in the definition of "all men" and "We the people," the proclamation helped to make their addition possible.

In part because of the postwar struggle of the freed people and their descendants, the proclamation has become a document of universal importance for the disadvantaged and oppressed beyond the black community and America's borders. Not that it is often invoked by the defenders of freedom or its provisions recalled. That degree of focus remains more academic than popular. Its importance rests, instead, in the fact that it ushered in the tradition of an expectation of equality and fairness. And that tradition has inspired others to press for the rights that freedmen and freedwomen and their descendants anticipated.

But regard for Lincoln has not stopped at America's shores. The legacy touches every corner of the globe. It is grounded in the presumption that all are entitled to human dignity and control over their destiny and that race, creed, origin, gender, and cultural preferences should not hinder the ability of the individual to pursue his or her own course.

Of course, the legacy is not Lincoln's alone. All those freed people who imbued his proclamation with meaning far beyond what most nineteenth-century Americans had intended share it. As their expectations soared, so did their possibilities. Lincoln's decree promised freedom; African Americans defined what that meant.

ACKNOWLEDGMENTS
NOTES
BIBLIOGRAPHY
INDEX

ACKNOWLEDGMENTS

I thank Sylvia Frank Rodrigue, Sara Vaughn Gabbard, and Richard Etulain for inviting me to contribute to the Concise Lincoln Library series. Writing even a succinct volume takes time, something a department chair rarely has. My editors understood the harried life of a scholar/administrator and exhibited infinite patience as I missed a deadline or two. Their careful review of the manuscript identified minor inconsistencies and more major concerns that I had missed. The comments provided by the outside reader convinced me to expand certain areas of the study that merited greater attention. And the expert reading of the manuscript by Daniel Stowell and his staff of the Abraham Lincoln Papers materially assisted me in producing a better volume. The efforts of all are greatly appreciated. Any imperfections that remain are in spite of their good counsel.

My graduate Civil War classes have always given me the opportunity to reexamine old ideas and consider new perspectives. I am especially grateful to my students for their enthusiasm for the era. They have kept me energized (and scrambling to keep up).

As always, I thank my daughter, Lark, for her technological assistance. And finally, I thank my husband, Thomas, for his insight and for his usual, unstinting support.

NOTES

Introduction

1. Quoted in Schwarz, *Gabriel's Conspiracy*, xv–xvi.
2. See Aptheker, *American Negro Slave Revolts*.
3. See Scully, *Religion and the Making of Nat Turner's Virginia*.
4. Two of the better-known critiques of Lincoln's actions and motivations can be found in Bennett, *Forced into Glory*, and DiLorenzo, *Real Lincoln*. Bennett argues that Lincoln was attempting to preserve slavery, and if he had been successful, the institution would have survived into the twentieth century. DiLorenzo sees Lincoln as a calculating politician who undermined the Constitution by crushing both individual and states' rights and by broadening the power of the national government. The attack on slavery was meant to further that end.
5. Guelzo, *Lincoln's Emancipation Proclamation*, 3–8.
6. In *Act of Justice*, Burrus Carnahan focuses on legal precedents regarding the emancipation of enslaved people during times of war. He argues that Lincoln took time to develop his rationale for decreeing freedom so as to garner the support of northerners as well as to shape and win international opinion.
7. J. Oakes, *Freedom National*, xii. See also his *Scorpion's Sting*.
8. According to Orville Vernon Burton, the Lincoln years witnessed the nation's struggle to define liberty and equality of opportunity as it pushed to perfect the democracy that had expanded (for white men) in the first half of the nineteenth century. See *Age of Lincoln*, 3–5.

1. The Man and His Times

1. Tocqueville, *Democracy in America*, 658–59.
2. Ibid., 303–6.
3. Ibid., 709.
4. Ibid., 385.
5. Ibid., 409.
6. Ibid., 385–86, 413, 416.
7. Ibid., 416–17. See also Litwack, *North of Slavery*.
8. Quoted in Foner and Branham, *Lift Every Voice*, 178–79.
9. Bell, *Minutes*.
10. Mayer, *All on Fire*.
11. Scully, *Religion and the Making of Nat Turner's Virginia*, 196. See also S. Oates, *Fires of Jubilee*.
12. Bartelt, *There I Grew Up*, 12.

13. Sandburg, *Abraham Lincoln*, 9.

14. Bartelt, *There I Grew Up*, 9, 12; Donald, *Lincoln*, 24.

15. Bartelt, *There I Grew Up*, 12.

16. Herndon and Weik, *Life of Lincoln*, 64.

17. Elmer Gertz, "Black Laws of Illinois," *Journal of the Illinois State Historical Society* 56, no. 3 (Autumn 1963): 461–63.

18. See Zabina Eastman, "Black Codes of Illinois," *Internet Archive: Digital Library of Free Books*, Library of the University of Illinois, https://archive.org/stream/blackcodeofillinooeast/blackcodeofillinooeast_djvu.txt.

19. Cassidy, "Issue of Freedom," 284–88.

20. Donald, *Lincoln*, 63–64.

21. Lincoln, "Protest in Illinois Legislature on Slavery," March 3, 1837, *Collected Works*, 1:75.

22. Clay, *Life and Speeches*, 2:597–98.

23. Clay, *Private Correspondence of Henry Clay*, 476–77.

24. Lincoln, "The Repeal of the Missouri Compromise and the Propriety of Its Restoration: Speech at Peoria, Illinois, in Reply to Senator Douglas, October 16, 1854," in Basler, *Abraham Lincoln*, 289.

25. See Ricks, *Escape on the* Pearl.

26. Lincoln, "Remarks and Resolution Introduced in the United States House of Representatives Concerning Abolition of Slavery in the District of Columbia," January 10, 1849, *Collected Works*, 2:20–22.

27. E. Foner, *Fiery Trial*, 46.

28. People v. Hill, *The Law Practice of Abraham Lincoln*, www.lawpracticeofabrahamlincoln.org.

29. Shelby v. Freeman and Freeman, Florville v. Allin et al., and Florville v. Stockdale et al., ibid.

30. In re Bryant et al., ibid. See also E. Foner, *Fiery Trial*, 48–50.

31. Lincoln, "Speech at Peoria, Illinois," October 16, 1854, *Collected Works*, 2:274–75.

32. According to David Donald, Lincoln was reticent to engage in debate at that time because he was concerned about the harm it might do to Whig chances to elect a president. See Donald, *Lincoln*, 134–35.

33. Lincoln, "Speech at Peoria, Illinois," *Collected Works*, 2:255.

34. Ibid., 2:268.

35. Ibid., 2:256, 268.

36. "The Fugitive Slave Act, 1850," *The Avalon Project: Documents in Law, History and Diplomacy*, http://avalon.law.yale.edu/19th_century/fugitive.asp.

37. P. Foner, *Voice of Black America*, 96–97.

38. See Fehrenbacher, *Slavery, Law, and Politics*.

39. Lincoln, "Speech at Springfield, Illinois," June 26, 1857, *Collected Works*, 2:403, 405–6, 406, 408–9.

40. Douglass, "The Dred Scott Decision," speech delivered before the American Anti-Slavery Society, New York, May 11, 1857, *Life and Writings*, 2:411; "The Final Triumph of Our Principles," *National Era*, May 14, 1857, www.accessible.com. All newspaper sources are from *Accessible Archives Database*, unless otherwise noted.

41. *Provincial Freeman*, March 28, 1857.

42. "Enquiry No. 2," ibid., April 11, 1857.

43. "Meetings at Philadelphia," ibid., April 18, 1857.

44. "Fruits of the Dred Scott Decision," *National Era*, May 7, 1857; "The Dred Scott Decision in Chicago," ibid., April 30, 1857; "Judge Taney's Dred Scott Decision," ibid., June 18, 1857.

45. Lincoln, "Speech at Charleston," September 18, 1858, *Collected Works*, 3:145–46.

2. The 1860 Election and the Loss of Union

1. Lincoln, "Notes on Speech in Kansas and Ohio, September 16–17, 1859," transcribed and annotated by the Lincoln Studies Center, Knox College, Galesburg, Ill., available at *Abraham Lincoln Papers at the Library of Congress*, http://memory.loc.gov/ammem/alhtml/alhome.html (hereafter *Lincoln Papers*, LC).

2. Holzer, *Lincoln at Cooper Union*, 10, 23–24. Holzer argues that the likely reason for moving the venue from Plymouth Church to Cooper Union was that the church's lecture season had ended.

3. Lincoln, "Address at Cooper Institute," February 27, 1860, *Collected Works*, 3:550.

4. Lincoln to Samuel Galloway, March 24, 1860, ibid., 4:34.

5. Donald, *Lincoln*, 244–50.

6. "Democratic Party Platform," 1860 Presidential Election, *The Avalon Project*, http://avalon.law.yale.edu/19th_century.

7. "National Democratic (Breckinridge) Platform," *Nineteenth Century Documents Project*, Furman University, http://history.furman.edu/benson/docs/bdemplat.htm.

8. "Constitutional Union Party Platform of 1860," May 9, 1860, *The American Presidency Project*, http://www.presidency.ucsb.edu/ws/?pid=29571.

9. "The Two Great Political Parties," *Weekly Anglo-African*, March 17, 1860 (microfilm). See also Ripley, *Black Abolitionist Papers*, 5:71–73.

10. H. Ford Douglas, "Speech at Framingham, July 4, 1860," *Liberator*, July 13, 1860.

11. Douglass, *Life and Writings*, 2:514–515.

12. Ibid., 2:484.

13. E. Foner, *Fiery Trial*, 140–44.

14. "Confederate States of America—Declaration of the Immediate Causes Which Induce and Justify the Secession of South Carolina from the Federal Union," *The Avalon Project*, http://avalon.law.yale.edu/19th_century/csa_scarsec.asp.

15. "A Declaration of the Immediate Causes Which Induce and Justify the Secession of the State of Mississippi from the Federal Union," ibid., http://avalon.law.yale.edu/19th_century/csa_missec.asp.

16. For a discussion on the intentions of the Republican Party, see J. Oakes, *Freedom National*.

17. Holzer, *Lincoln, President-Elect*, 163–64.

18. Lincoln to Lyman Trumbull, December 10, 1860, *Collected Works*, 4:149.

19. Lincoln to Gen. Duff Green, December 28, 1860, ibid., 4:162.

20. Lincoln to William H. Seward, February 1, 1861, ibid., 4:183.

21. Holzer, *Lincoln, President-Elect*, 427–29.

22. "Lincoln, "First Inaugural Address," March 4, 1861, *Collected Works*, 4:263, 266, 270.

23. "The Declaration of War," *Richmond Enquirer*, March 5, 1861; "The Inaugural Address of President Lincoln," *Charleston Mercury*, March 5, 1861; "The Inaugural Address of Mr. Lincoln—The Country No Wiser," *New York Herald*, March 5, 1861; "Opinions of the Abolition Press," *Charleston Mercury*, March 9, 1861.

24. Douglass, "The Inaugural Address," *Frederick Douglass*, 434–35; *Weekly Anglo-African*, March 16, 1861.

25. Douglass, "The Union and How to Save It," *Frederick Douglass*, 429–31.

26. Quoted in McPherson, *Negro's Civil War*, 11.

27. Thomas Hamilton, "Editorial," December 22, 1860, in Ripley, *Black Abolitionist Papers*, 5:98–99.

3. War, Union, and Slavery

1. "Proclamation Calling Militia and Convening Congress," April 15, 1861, *Collected Works*, 4:331–33.

2. "The Appeal to Arms—President Lincoln's War Manifesto," *New York Herald*, April 15, 1861; "The War Begun!," *Weekly Vincennes Western Sun*, April 20, 1861; *Vincennes Gazette*, April 20, 1861.

3. "What of the Night," *Weekly Anglo-African*, April 20, 1861; "Virginia's Punishment," ibid., April 27, 1861 (microfilm).

4. "Editorials by George Lawrence, Jr.," in Ripley, *Black Abolitionist Papers*, 5:111.

5. "Attack on the Constitution," *Weekly Anglo-African*, April 27, 1861; Quarles, *Negro in the Civil War*, 29.

6. Douglass, "The Future of the Negro people of the Slave States," February 5, 1862, in *Frederick Douglass*, 476.

7. "Facts for Patriotic Abolitionists," *Weekly Anglo-African*, May 11, 1861.

8. "Have We a War Policy," ibid., April 27, 1861; October 19, 1861.

9. "Speech of Mr. B. K. Sampson," quoted in ibid., November 9, 1861.

10. Davis, *Battle at Bull Run*.

11. Douglass, "Dissolution of the American Union," *Frederick Douglass*, 427–28.

12. Lieutenant A. J. Slemmer to Lt. Col. Lorenzo Thomas, Assistant Adjutant-General, March 18, 1861, *The War of the Rebellion: A Compilation of the Official Records of the Union and Confederate Armies*, 128 vols. (Washington: Government Printing Office, 1880–1901), ser. 2, 1:750 (hereafter *OR*).

13. Benj. F. Butler to Lieut. Gen. Winfield Scott, May 24, 1861, ibid., ser. 2, 1:752. See also *Negro in Virginia*, 210.

14. Edward L. Pierce, "The Contrabands at Fortress Monroe," *Atlantic Monthly*, November 1861, 627–30.

15. Charles B. Calvert to Abraham Lincoln, July 10, 1861, *Lincoln Papers*, LC; Lieutenant Colonel Schuyler Hamilton to Brigadier General Irwin McDowell, Washington, July 16, 1861, *OR*, ser. 2, 1:760.

16. "Letter from Rev. J. Sella Martin," *Douglass' Monthly*, June 1861.

17. Douglass, *Life and Writings*, 3:105.

18. Orson S. Murray to the Editor, "Be Not Deceived—Be Not Mocked," *Liberator*, May 31, 1861.

19. Donald, *Lincoln*, 314. James Oakes argues that Lincoln was reluctant to sign the First Confiscation Act because he was concerned that such action would signal a larger plan of emancipation. See *Freedom National*, 137.

20. Donald, *Lincoln*, 314.

21. Lincoln to John C. Frémont, September 2, 1861, and September 11, 1861, *Collected Works*, 4:506, 518.

22. Henry Jones to Abraham Lincoln, September 24, 1861, *Lincoln Papers*, LC.

23. William R. Prince to Abraham Lincoln, September 20, 1861, ibid.

24. Charles Reed to Abraham Lincoln, Tuesday, September 24, 1861, ibid.

25. O. B. Clark and John Root, Resolutions, Tuesday, September 17, 1861, ibid.

26. "No Backward Step," *Christian Recorder*, September 28, 1861.

27. Douglass, "General Frémont's Proclamation to the Rebels of Missouri," *Douglass' Monthly*, October 1861, in *Life and Writings*, 3:160–61.

28. Charles S. Homer to Abraham Lincoln, September 17, 1861, *Lincoln Papers*, LC.

29. Douglass, "Frémont and Freedom—Lincoln and Slavery," *Douglass' Monthly*, November 1861 (microfilm).

30. Orville H. Browning to Abraham Lincoln, September 17, 1861, *Lincoln Papers*, LC.

31. Lincoln to Orville H. Browning, September 22, 1861, *Collected Works*, 4:531.

32. Lincoln, "Drafts of Bill for Compensated Emancipation in Delaware," *Abraham Lincoln*, 276–77.

33. Soodalter, *Hanging Captain Gordon*, 34–35.

34. "The Execution of Gordon, the Slave-Trader," March 8, 1862, *Toward Racial Equality: Harper's Weekly Reports on Black America, 1857–1874*, http://blackhistory.harpweek.com/7Illustrations/Slavery/ExecutionOfSlavetrader.htm. See also "The Execution of Nathaniel Gordon," *New York Times*, February 22, 1862, http://nytimes.com/1862/02/22/news/the-execution-ofnathaniel-gordon.html.

35. Ron Soodalter, "Hanging Captain Gordon," August 18, 2009, www.historynet.com/hanging-captain-gordon.htm.

36. Lincoln, "Stay of Execution for Nathaniel Gordon," *Collected Works*, 5:128.

37. "The Hanging of Gordon for Man-stealing," *Weekly Anglo-African*, March 1, 1862.

38. Lincoln, "Message to Congress," March 6, 1862, *Collected Works*, 5:144–45.

39. "An Act to Make an Additional Article of War, March 13, 1862," *Freedmen and Southern Society Project*, http://www.freedmen.umd.edu/milact.htm.

40. "The District of Columbia Emancipation Act," National Archives and Records Administration, http://www.archives.gov/exhibits/featured_documents/dc_emancipation_act.

41. "District of Columbia Emancipation Act, Supplemental Act of July 12, 1862," ibid.

42. Browning, *Diary of Orville Hickman Browning*, 1:541.

43. Lincoln, "Message to Congress," April 16, 1862, *Collected Works*, 5:192.

44. Browning, *Diary of Orville Hickman Browning*, 1:541.

45. Lincoln, "Message to Congress," April 16, 1862, *Collected Works*, 5:192.

46. J. Oakes, *Freedom National*, 265–69. Oakes considers the abolition of slavery in the territories a crucial stage in the Republican Party's quest for universal emancipation.

47. Chapter 111, "An Act to Secure Freedom to all Persons within the Territories of the United States," approved June 19, 1862, 37th Congress, 2nd Session, Laws of the United States, appendix to the *Congressional Globe*, June 20, 1862, 364.

48. Lincoln, "Message to the Senate and House of Representatives," July 17, 1862, *Collected Works*, 5:331. See also U.S. Constitution, art. III, sec. 3.

49. "The Militia Act of 1862," *Freedmen and Southern Society Project.*

50. Lincoln, "Proclamation Revoking General Hunter's Order of Military Emancipation," May 19, 1862, *Collected Works*, 5:222–23.

51. Lincoln, "Appeal to Border State Representatives to Favor Compensated Emancipation," July 12, 1862, ibid., 5:317–18.

52. "Memorial to the President from the Religious Society of Progressive Friends."

53. Lincoln, "Remarks to a Delegation of Progressive Friends," June 20, 1862, *Collected Works*, 5:278–79.

54. Lincoln, "Remarks to Committee of Reformed Presbyterian Synod," July 17, 1862, ibid., 5:327.

55. Lincoln, "Reply to Emancipation Memorial Presented by Chicago Christians of All Denominations," ibid., 5:419–25.

56. Burrus Carnahan argues that Lincoln's delay in issuing the Emancipation Proclamation resulted from his concern that international and national forces recognized that military necessity. Otherwise, the decree stood a greater chance of being challenged. See *Act of Justice*, 141.

57. Donald, *Lincoln*, 364; see also Goodwin, *Team of Rivals*, 463–68.

58. Goodwin, *Team of Rivals*, 467–68.

59. See Dixon, *African Americans and Haiti.*

60. K. Masur, "African American Delegation," 123.

61. Quoted in McPherson, *Negro's Civil War*, 92.

62. John Rock, "Speech of John Rock at the Annual Meeting of the Massachusetts Anti-Slavery Society," January 28, 1862, *Liberator*, February 14, 1862.

63. K. Masur, "African American Delegation," 126–27.

64. Ibid., 130–31. See also Ripley, *Black Abolitionist Papers*, 141n, 155n. Masur dispels the myth that all but one of the five men had been recently enslaved.

65. Lincoln, "Address on Colonization to a Deputation of Negroes," August 14, 1862, *Collected Works*, 5:372.

66. Douglass, "The President and His Speeches," September 1862, *Frederick Douglass*, 511.

67. Quoted in McPherson, *Negro's Civil War*, 95.

68. Frances Ellen Watkins Harper, "Mrs. Frances E. Watkins Harper on the War and the President's Colonization Scheme," *Christian Recorder*, September 27, 1862.

69. "George B. Vashon to Abraham Lincoln," September 1862, in Ripley, *Black Abolitionist Papers*, 152–55.

70. Horace Greeley, "The Prayer of Twenty Millions," *New York Tribune*, August 19, 1862 (microfilm).

71. Lincoln to Horace Greeley, August 22, 1862, *Collected Works*, 5:388–89.

72. "Reply to Emancipation Memorial Presented by Chicago Christians of All Denominations," September 13, 1862, ibid., 5:419–21.

4. Emancipation by Presidential Decree

1. Lincoln, "The Preliminary Emancipation Proclamation," September 22, 1862, *Collected Works*, 5:433–36.

2. Resolutions of the Confederate Congress, introduced by Senator Thomas J. Semmes, September 29, 1862, *Journal of the Congress of the Confederate States of America, 1861–1865*, 2:375, quoted in the *Liberator*, October 17, 1862, and the *New York Times*, October 4, 1862.

3. Quoted in "Selections: Et Tu Brute," *Liberator*, October 17, 1862.

4. "Reported Negro Plot in Virginia," *Christian Recorder*, October 25, 1862; see also "Reported Insurrectionary Movements in Culpeper and Adjoining Counties," *National Republican*, October 20, 1862.

5. *New York Independent* and *Hartford Courant* quoted in "The Press on the President's Emancipation Proclamation," *Liberator*, October 3, 1862.

6. "The Proclamation," *Christian Recorder*, October 18, 1862.

7. Donald, *Lincoln*, 385–90; Klingaman, *Abraham Lincoln*, 203–4, 217–18.

8. *New York Express* and *Boston Courier* quoted in "The Proclamation," *Liberator*, October 3, 1862.

9. Donald, *Lincoln*, 378–80; Klingaman, *Abraham Lincoln*, 198–99.

10. "The 'Cry for a Policy' Obeyed" and *Louisville Journal* quoted in *Weekly Vincennes Western Sun*, September 27, 1862.

11. Weber, *Copperheads*, 64; Long, *Jewel of Liberty*, 45.

12. Douglass, *Life and Writings*, 3:294–95.

13. Donald, *Lincoln*, 282–83.

14. Lord Palmerston quoted in Guelzo, "How Abe Lincoln Lost the Black Vote," 3.

15. Quoted in Mitgang, *Abraham Lincoln, a Press Portrait*, 320.

16. Douglass, *Life and Writings*, 3:309.

17. Lincoln, "Annual Message to Congress," December 1, 1862, *Collected Works*, 5:531.

18. Lincoln, "The Final Emancipation Proclamation," January 1, 1863, ibid., 6:30.

19. Lincoln, Preliminary Draft of Final Emancipation Proclamation (annotation), *Collected Works*, 6:25.

20. Douglass, *Autobiographies*, 791–92.

21. "Grand Emancipation Jubilee," *New York Times*, January 1, 1863 (microfilm).

22. Quoted in Sterling, *Speak Out in Thunder Tones*, 316.

23. "Rev. Henry Ward Beecher on the President's Proclamation and the Present Crisis," *New York Times*, January 6, 1863.

24. Douglass, *Life and Writings*, 3:321.

25. Ibid., 3:323.

26. "Short Comings, and Worse," *Liberator*, January 16, 1863.

27. "The Emancipation Proclamation—The Last Card of the Abolition Programme," *New York Herald*, January 3, 1863.

28. "The Proclamation," *Weekly Vincennes Western Sun*, January 10, 1863.

29. *Daily Illinois State Register*, January 6, 1863. See also *Daily Illinois State Journal*, January 7, 1863, Abraham Lincoln Presidential Library and Museum (microfilm), Springfield, Ill.

30. *Louisville Democrat* quoted in "The Proclamation," *Weekly Vincennes Western Sun*, January 10, 1863.

31. "Lincoln's Proclamation," *Daily Dispatch* (Richmond, VA), January 6, 1863.

32. Jefferson Davis, "Address to the Senate and House of Representatives of the Confederate States," January 12, 1863, *Journal of the Congress of the Confederate States of America, 1861–1865*, 3:13.

5. To Know Freedom

1. *New York Tribune* quoted in "Don't Want to Be Free!" *Liberator*, April 3, 1863.

2. Sterling, *We Are Your Sisters*, 243.

3. Blassingame, *Slave Testimony*, 616–18.

4. For a discussion of recruitment in the border states, see Berlin et al., *Free at Last*, 341–59.

5. Interview of Henri Necaise in Yetman, *Life under the Peculiar Institution*, 238.

6. Hughes, *Thirty Years a Slave*, 126.

7. "The Negro Question in Texas," *New York Times*, July 9, 1865, http://www.nytimes.com/1865/07/09/news/the-negro-question-in-texas.

8. "Negroes in Mississippi," *Christian Recorder*, January 3, 1863; *Douglass' Monthly*, February 1863.

9. Lincoln to Charles D. Robinson, August 17, 1864, *Collected Works*, 7:500.

10. Charles Wilder, Testimony Before the American Freedmen's Inquiry Commission, May 9, 1863, in Berlin et al., *Free at Last*, 107–10.

11. Reidy, "'Coming from the Shadow of the Past,'" 411. On the contraband camp at Corinth, see Blight, *Slave No More*, 151.

12. Sterling, *We Are Your Sisters*, 245.

13. Quoted in Marten, *Children's Civil War*, 113.

14. Keckley, *Behind the Scenes*, 114, 116.

15. Berlin et al., *Free at Last*, 192–97.

16. Lincoln, "Annual Message to Congress," December 8, 1863, *Collected Works*, 7:49–50.

17. Berlin et al., *Free at Last*, 435. See also Smith, *Lincoln and the United States Colored Troops*.

18. Lincoln, "Reply to Chicago Emancipation Memorial," Washington, D.C., September 13, 1862, *Abraham Lincoln*, 365.

19. John A. Andrew to George T. Downing, March 23, 1863, in Berlin et al., *Free at Last*, 436–37.

20. Douglass, "Our Work is Not Done," *Frederick Douglass*, 551–52.

21. Lincoln, "Annual Message to Congress," December 8, 1863, *Collected Works*, 7:50.

22. Lincoln to James C. Conkling, August 26, 1863, ibid., 6:408–9.

23. Litwack, *Been in the Storm So Long*, 94–95.

24. Blassingame, *Slave Testimony*, 586.

25. Berlin and Rowland, *Families and Freedom*, 32.

26. Ibid., 32.

27. John J. Pettus, Governor and Commander-in-Chief, to Gentlemen of the Senate and House of Representatives, November 3, 1863, *OR*, ser. 4, 2:922.

28. Governor Charles Clark to Fellow Citizens, Executive Office, Columbus, Mississippi, November 16, 1863, ibid., 2:960–61.

29. Louisiana Planters to the Commander of the Department of the Gulf, January 14, 1863, *Freedmen and Southern Society Project*, http://www.history.umd.edu/Freedmen/minor.htm.

30. Maj. Gen. Lovell H. Rousseau to Brig. Gen. W. D. Whipple, January 30, 1864, *OR*, ser. 1, 32:267.

31. Berlin et al., *Free at Last*, 116.

32. George W. Hatton to the *Christian Recorder*, May 28, 1864.

33. Berlin et al., *Free at Last*, 116.

34. Seager, *And Tyler Too*, 490–91.

35. Blassingame, *Slave Testimony*, 465.

36. Lincoln to John A. McClernand, January 8, 1863; Lincoln to Nathaniel P. Banks, August 5, 1863; Lincoln to Nathaniel P. Banks, November 5, 1863, all in *Collected Works*, 6:48–49, 364, 7:1–2.

37. Lincoln, "Message to Congress," December 1863, ibid., 7:51.

38. "Louisiana Planters to the Commander of the Department of the Gulf," January 14, 1863, *Freedom and Southern Society Project*.

39. Minutes of an interview between the Colored Ministers and Church Officers at Savannah with the Secretary of War and Major-Gen. Sherman, January 12, 1865, in Berlin et al., *Free at Last*, 310–18.

40. McPherson, *Negro's Civil War*, 300.

41. Don Carlos Rutter dictated his letter to Laura Towne. Laura Towne to Abraham Lincoln, Sunday, May 29, 1864, *Lincoln Papers*, LC.

42. Berlin et al., *Freedom*, 338-40.

43. Howard, *Autobiography*, 2:237–38.

44. Louisiana Freedmen to the Provost Marshal General of the Department of the Gulf, and Statement of the Commander of Camp Hoyt, Louisiana, Terre Bonne Parish, April 5, 1863, in Berlin et al., *Free at Last*, 257–58.

45. Berlin et al., *Free at Last*, 502.

46. Lincoln to Michael Hahn, March 13, 1864, *Collected Works*, 7:243.

47. Lincoln, "Last Public Address," April 11, 1865, ibid., 8:403–4.

6. Ending Slavery Forever

1. Lincoln to John A. McClernand, January 8, 1863, *Collected Works*, 6:48–49; Lincoln to James Conkling, August 26, 1863, ibid., 6:406–10.

2. Lincoln, "Proclamation of Amnesty and Reconstruction," December 8, 1863, ibid., 7:54.

3. E. Foner, *Fiery Trial*, 291.

4. "Amendment of the Constitution," December 14, 1863, *Congressional Globe*, 38th Congress, 1st Session, 19, http://memory.loc.gov/ammem/amlaw/wcglink.html.

5. Ibid.; "Amendment Proposed by Senator Charles Sumner," April 8, 1864, ibid., 1483.

6. "Speech of Senator Lyman Trumbull in favor of the Constitutional Amendment," March 28, 1864, ibid., 1314.

7. Vorenberg, *Final Freedom*, 96–97.

8. Quoted in E. Foner, *Fiery Trial*, 293.

9. The new Democracy Party consisted of disaffected Radical Republicans who supported John Frémont.

10. Lincoln to John D. Defrees, February 8, 1864, *Collected Works*, 7:172. Lincoln's reply appears as an endorsement on the letter that Defrees had written to him the day before.

11. "Republican Party Platform of 1864," June 7, 1864, *The American Presidency Project*, http://www.presidency.ucsb.edu/ws/print.php?pid=29621.

12. "Reply to Committee Notifying Lincoln of His Re-nomination," June 9, 1864, *Collected Works*, 7:380.

13. "Democratic Party Platform of 1864," *The American Presidency Project*, http://www.presidency.ucsb.edu/ws/print.php?pid=29578.

14. Douglass, *Autobiographies*, 795–96.

15. "'Africano' to Robert Hamilton," in Ripley, *Black Abolitionist Papers*, 277–78.

16. Stevens, *Congressional Globe*, 38th Congress, 2nd Session, 265.

17. Henry Highland Garnet, "Let the Monster Perish," speech delivered in the House of Representatives Chamber, February 12, 1865, in Foner and Branham, *Lift Every Voice*, 432–45.

18. Douglass, "The Need for Continuing Anti-Slavery Work," *Frederick Douglass*, 578–79.

19. Lincoln, "Second Inaugural Address," March 4, 1865, *Collected Works*, 8:332–33.

20. Douglass, *Autobiographies*, 804.

Epilogue

1. "Our Loss," *New York Herald*, April 16, 1865.

2. "Sadness," ibid., April 19, 1865.

3. "Letter from Bloomington," *Christian Recorder*, April 29, 1865; "Letter from California," ibid., May 20, 1865.

4. Quarles, *Lincoln and the Negro*, 245.

5. "Monument to President Lincoln," *Christian Recorder*, May 20, 1865.

6. Quarles, *Lincoln and the Negro*, 4.

7. Quoted in Edna Greene Medford, "Imagined Promises, Bitter Realities: African Americans and the Meaning of the Emancipation Proclamation," in Holzer, Medford, and Williams, *Emancipation Proclamation*, 37.

8. Quoted in Quarles, *Lincoln and the Negro*, 4.

9. J. J. Hill quoted in Aptheker, *Documentary History of the Negro*, 489–90.

10. Douglass at Cooper Union, June 1, 1865, Frederick Douglass Papers, LC.

11. Frederick Douglass, "Oration in Memory of Abraham Lincoln, delivered at the unveiling of the Freedmen's Monument," April 14, 1876, *Frederick Douglass*, 618–19.

12. "Grand Celebration," *Christian Recorder*, September 15, 1866; "Emancipation Anniversary," ibid., September 11, 1869.

13. "The Freedmen's Celebration," ibid., July 29, 1865.

14. Booker T. Washington, "An Address on Abraham Lincoln," February 12, 1909, before the Republican Club of New York City, in *Selected Speeches of Booker T. Washington*, 195.

15. Quoted in Dunbar-Nelson, *Masterpieces of Negro Eloquence*, 332–33.

16. Quoted in Yetman, *Life under the Peculiar Institution*, 238.

17. Quoted in Ward, *Slaves' War*, 252.

18. Quoted in Mellon, *Bullwhip Days*, 459.

19. Quoted in Williams, *Weren't No Good Times*, 57, 61.

20. Sallie Paul, WPA interview, November 19, 1937, *Born in Slavery: Slave Narratives from the Federal Writers' Project, 1936–1938*, http://memory.loc.gov/cgi-bin/ampge?collid=mesn&filName=143/m.

21. Quoted in Meyer, *Myths in Stone*, 219–20.

22. Martin L. King Jr., "I Have a Dream," March on Washington for Jobs and Freedom, August 28, 1963, National Archives and Records Administration, www.archive.gov/press/exhibits/dream.

BIBLIOGRAPHY

Aptheker, Herbert, ed. *American Negro Slave Revolts*. New York: International Publishers, 1993.

———. *A Documentary History of the Negro People in the United States: From Colonial Times through the Civil War*. Vol. 1. New York: Citadel Press, 1965.

Bartelt, William E. *There I Grew Up: Remembering Abraham Lincoln's Indiana Youth*. Indianapolis: Indiana Historical Society Press, 2008.

Basler, Roy P., ed. *Abraham Lincoln: His Speeches and Writings*. New York: Da Capo Press, 1990.

Bell, Howard H. *Minutes of the Proceedings of the National Negro Conventions, 1830–1864*. New York: Arno Press, 1969.

Bennett, Lerone. *Forced into Glory: Abraham Lincoln's White Dream*. Chicago: Johnson Publishing, 2000.

Berlin, Ira. *Slaves without Masters: The Free Negro in the Antebellum South*. New York: Oxford University Press, 1974.

Berlin, Ira, Barbara J. Fields, Steven F. Miller, Joseph P. Reidy, and Leslie Rowland, eds. *Free at Last: A Documentary History of Slavery, Freedom and the Civil War*. New York: New Press, 1992.

Berlin, Ira, Thavolia Glymph, Steven F. Miller, Joseph P. Reidy, Leslie S. Rowland, and Julie Saville. *The Wartime Genesis of Free Labor: The Lower South*. Vol. 3, ser. 1, *Freedom: A Documentary History of Emancipation, 1861–1867*. New York: Cambridge University Press, 1991.

Berlin, Ira, and Leslie Rowland, eds. *Families and Freedom: A Documentary History of African-American Kinship in the Civil War Era*. New York: New Press, 1997.

Blassingame, John W., ed. *Slave Testimony: Two Centuries of Letters, Speeches, Interviews, and Autobiographies*. Baton Rouge: Louisiana State University Press, 1977.

Blight, David. *A Slave No More: Two Men Who Escaped to Freedom, Including Their Own Narratives of Emancipation*. Boston: Houghton Mifflin, 2007.

Browning, Orville H. *The Diary of Orville Hickman Browning*. Edited with introduction and notes by Thomas Calvin Pease and James G. Randall. 2 vols. Springfield: Trustees of the Illinois Historical Library, 1925–33.

Burlingame, Michael. *Abraham Lincoln: A Life*. 2 vols. Baltimore: Johns Hopkins University Press, 2008.

Burton, Orville Vernon. *The Age of Lincoln*. New York: Hill and Wang, 2007.

Carnahan, Burrus M. *Act of Justice: Lincoln's Emancipation Proclamation and the Law of War*. Lexington: University of Kentucky Press, 2007.

Carpenter, Francis B. *Six Months in the White House with Abraham Lincoln*. Ann Arbor: University of Michigan Press, 2005.

Cassidy, John Thomas. "The Issue of Freedom in Illinois under Gov. Edward Coles, 1822–1826." *Journal of the Illinois State Historical Society* 57 (1964): 284–97.

Clay, Henry. *The Life and Speeches of the Hon. Henry Clay.* Compiled and edited by Daniel Mallory. 2 vols. New York: A. S. Barnes, 1853.

———. *The Private Correspondence of Henry Clay.* Edited by Calvin Colton. New York: A. S. Barnes and Company, 1855.

Davis, William C. *Battle at Bull Run: The First Major Campaign of the Civil War.* Baton Rouge: Louisiana State University Press, 1995.

DiLorenzo, Thomas. *The Real Lincoln: A New Look at Abraham Lincoln, His Agenda, and an Unnecessary War.* New York: Three Rivers Press, 2003.

Dixon, Chris. *African Americans and Haiti: Emigration and Black Nationalism in the Nineteenth Century.* New York: Praeger, 2000.

Donald, David Herbert. *Lincoln.* New York: Simon and Schuster, 1995.

Douglass, Frederick. *Autobiographies.* Edited by Henry Louis Gates Jr. New York: Library Company of America, 1994.

———. *Frederick Douglass: Selected Speeches and Writings.* Edited by Philip Foner and abridged by Yuval Taylor. Chicago: Lawrence Hill Books, 1999.

———. *The Life and Writings of Frederick Douglass.* Edited by Philip Foner. 4 vols. New York: International Publishers, 1987.

Dunbar-Nelson, Alice, ed. *Masterpieces of Negro Eloquence: The Best Speeches Delivered by the Negro from the Days of Slavery to the Present Time.* New York: Bookery Publishing Company, 1914.

Fehrenbacher, Don E. *Slavery, Law, and Politics: The Dred Scott Case in Historical Perspective.* New York: Oxford University Press, 1981.

Foner, Eric. *The Fiery Trial: Abraham Lincoln and American Slavery.* New York: W. W. Norton, 2010.

Foner, Philip S., ed. *The Voice of Black America: Major Speeches by Negroes in the United States, 1797–1971.* New York: Simon and Schuster, 1972.

Foner, Philip S., and Robert Branham. *Lift Every Voice: African American Oratory, 1787–1901.* Tuscaloosa: University of Alabama Press, 1998.

Franklin, John Hope. *The Emancipation Proclamation.* Garden City, NY: Doubleday, 1963.

Gates, Henry Louis, Jr., ed. *Lincoln on Race and Slavery.* Princeton: Princeton University Press, 2009.

Goodwin, Doris Kearns. *Team of Rivals: The Political Genius of Abraham Lincoln.* New York: Simon and Schuster, 2005.

Guelzo, Allen C. "How Abe Lincoln Lost the Black Vote: Lincoln and Emancipation in the African American Mind." *Journal of the Abraham Lincoln Association* 25, no. 1 (Winter 2004): 1–22.

——. *Lincoln's Emancipation Proclamation: The End of Slavery in America.* New York: Simon and Schuster, 2004.

Herndon, William H., and Jesse W. Weik. *Life of Lincoln.* New York: World Publishing, 1942 (reprint).

Holzer, Harold. *Lincoln at Cooper Union: The Speech That Made Abraham Lincoln President.* New York: Simon and Schuster, 2004.

——. *Lincoln, President-Elect: Abraham Lincoln and the Great Secession Winter, 1860–1861.* New York: Simon and Schuster, 2008.

Holzer, Harold, Edna Greene Medford, and Frank Williams. *The Emancipation Proclamation: Three Views.* Baton Rouge: Louisiana State University Press, 2006.

Howard, Oliver Otis. *The Autobiography of Oliver Otis Howard, Major General, United States Army.* 2 vols. New York: Baker and Taylor, 1907.

Hughes, Louis. *Thirty Years a Slave: From Bondage to Freedom.* Montgomery, AL: New South Books, 2002.

Keckley, Elizabeth. *Behind the Scenes: Or, Thirty Years a Slave, and Four Years in the White House.* New York: G. W. Carleton, 1868.

Klingaman, William K. *Abraham Lincoln and the Road to Emancipation.* New York: Penguin, 2001.

Lincoln, Abraham. *Abraham Lincoln: Speeches and Writings, 1859–1865.* Edited by Don E. Fehrenbacher. New York: Library of America, 2012.

——. *The Collected Works of Abraham Lincoln.* Edited by Roy P. Basler. 9 vols. New Brunswick, NJ: Rutgers University Press, 1953–55. Published under the auspices of the Abraham Lincoln Association and available online at http://quod.lib.umich.edu/l/lincoln.

Litwack, Leon F. *Been in the Storm So Long: The Aftermath of Slavery.* New York: Vintage, 1979.

——. *North of Slavery: The Negro in the Free States, 1790–1860.* Chicago: University of Chicago Press, 1961.

Long, David. *The Jewel of Liberty: Abraham Lincoln's Re-election and the End of Slavery.* Mechanicsburg, PA: Stackpole, 1994.

Magness, Philip W. *Colonization after Emancipation: Lincoln and the Movement for Black Resettlement.* Columbia: University of Missouri Press, 2011.

Marten, James A. *The Children's Civil War.* Chapel Hill: University of North Carolina Press, 2000.

Masur, Kate. "The African American Delegation to Abraham Lincoln: A Reappraisal." *Civil War History* 56 (2010): 117–44.

Masur, Louis P. *Lincoln's Hundred Days: The Emancipation Proclamation and the War for the Union.* Cambridge, MA: Belknap, 2012.

Mayer, Henry. *All on Fire: William Lloyd Garrison and the Abolition of Slavery.* New York: W. W. Norton, 1998.

McPherson, James M. *The Negro's Civil War: How American Blacks Felt and Acted during the War for the Union*. New York: Ballantine Books, 1991.

Mellon, James. *Bullwhip Days: The Slaves Remember*. New York: Grove Press, 1988.

"Memorial to the President from the Religious Society of Progressive Friends." In *Proceedings of the Pennsylvania Yearly Meeting of Progressive Friends, 1862*. New York: John Trow, 1862.

Meyer, Jeffrey. *Myths in Stone: Religious Dimensions of Washington*. Berkeley: University of California Press, 2001.

Mitgang, Herbert, ed. *Abraham Lincoln, a Press Portrait: His Life and Times from the Original Newspaper Documents of the Union, the Confederacy, and Europe*. New York: Fordham University Press, 2000.

Negro in Virginia. Compiled by workers of the Writers' Program of the Work Projects Administration in the State of Virginia. 1940; repr., Winston-Salem, NC: John F. Blair, 1994.

Oakes, James. *Freedom National: The Destruction of Slavery in the United States, 1861–1865*. New York: W. W. Norton, 2013.

———. *The Scorpion's Sting: Antislavery and the Coming of the Civil War*. New York: W. W. Norton, 2014.

Oates, Stephen. *The Fires of Jubilee: Nat Turner's Fierce Rebellion*. New York: Harper Perennial, 1990.

Peterson, Merrill D. *Lincoln in American Memory*. New York: Oxford University Press, 1994.

Pierson, George Wilson. *Tocqueville in America*. Baltimore: Johns Hopkins University Press, 1996.

Quarles, Benjamin. *Lincoln and the Negro*. New York: Da Capo Press, 1990.

———. *The Negro in the Civil War*. Boston: Little, Brown, 1969.

Reidy, Joseph P. "'Coming from the Shadow of the Past': The Transition from Slavery to Freedom at Freedmen's Village, 1863–1900." *Virginia Magazine of History and Biography* 95, no. 4 (October 1987): 403–28.

Ricks, Mary Kay. *Escape on the* Pearl*: The Heroic Bid for Freedom on the Underground Railroad*. New York: William Morrow, 2007.

Ripley, C. Peter, ed. *The Black Abolitionist Papers*. Vol. 5, *The United States 1859–1865*. Chapel Hill: University of North Carolina Press, 1992.

Sandburg, Carl. *Abraham Lincoln: The Prairie Years and the Civil War Years*. New York: Galahad Books, 1939.

Schwarz, Philip J., ed. *Gabriel's Conspiracy: A Documentary History*. Charlottesville: University of Virginia Press, 2012.

Scully, Randolph Ferguson. *Religion and the Making of Nat Turner's Virginia: Baptist Community and Conflict, 1740–1840*. Charlottesville: University of Virginia Press, 2008.

Seager, Robert, II. *And Tyler Too: A Biography of John and Julia Gardiner Tyler*. New York: McGraw Hill, 1963.

Smith, John David. *Lincoln and the United States Colored Troops*. Carbondale: Southern Illinois University Press, 2013.

Soodalter, Ron. *Hanging Captain Gordon: The Life and Trial of an American Slave Trader*. New York: Washington Square Press, 2006.

Sterling, Dorothy, ed. *Speak Out in Thunder Tones: Letters and Writings by Black Northerners, 1787–1865*. New York: Da Capo Press, 1998.

———, ed. *We Are Your Sisters: Black Women in the Nineteenth Century*. New York: W. W. Norton, 1984.

Tocqueville, Alexis de. *Democracy in America*. Trans. Henry Reeve. New York: Bantam Dell, 2000.

Vorenberg, Michael. *Final Freedom: The Civil War, the Abolition of Slavery, and the Thirteenth Amendment*. Cambridge: Cambridge University Press, 2001.

Ward, Andrew. *The Slaves' War: The Civil War in the Words of Former Slaves*. Boston: Houghton Mifflin, 2008.

Washington, Booker T. *Selected Speeches of Booker T. Washington*. Edited by E. David Washington. Garden City, NY: Doubleday, Dora, and Company, 1932.

Weber, Jennifer. *Copperheads: The Rise and Fall of Lincoln's Opposition in the North*. New York: Oxford University Press, 2006.

Williams, Horace Randall. *Weren't No Good Times: Personal Accounts of Slavery in Alabama*. New York: John Blair, 2004.

Yetman, Norman, ed. *Life under the Peculiar Institution*. New York: Holt, Rinehart, and Winston, 1970.

INDEX

Edna Greene Medford, a professor of history and associate provost for faculty affairs at Howard University in Washington, DC, specializes in mid- to late-nineteenth-century United States history, in particular the experiences of people of African descent in slavery and freedom. She is a coauthor, with Harold Holzer and Frank Williams, of *The Emancipation Proclamation: Three Views*.

CONCISE
LINCOLN
LIBRARY

This series of concise books fills a need for short studies of the life, times, and legacy of President Abraham Lincoln. Each book gives readers the opportunity to quickly achieve basic knowledge of a Lincoln-related topic. These books bring fresh perspectives to well-known topics, investigate previously overlooked subjects, and explore in greater depth topics that have not yet received book-length treatment. For a complete list of current and forthcoming titles, see www.conciselincolnlibrary.com.

Other Books in the Concise Lincoln Library

Lincoln and Religion
Ferenc Morton Szasz with
Margaret Connell Szasz

*Lincoln and the Natural
Environment*
James Tackach

Lincoln and the War's End
John C. Waugh

Lincoln as Hero
Frank J. Williams

Abraham and Mary Lincoln
Kenneth J. Winkle